The HOUSE *on* HATHAWAY ROAD

WHERE MEMORIES BEGAN

Aventine Press

Published by Aventine Press
55 East Emerson St.
Chula Vista CA, 91911
www.aventinepress.com

1-59330-812-4

Printed in the United States of America

Acknowledgements

William H. Henkaline and Olive O. Henkaline

The most important purpose of sharing our Memories is to express our heartfelt love and devotion for our wonderful parents and to acknowledge their unselfish examples of parenthood. We are extremely thankful that they took important time to lovingly nurture and direct us in Christian Principles.

Jack Henkaline

The siblings of "Jack Blaine", our self appointed Family Activities Director want to give our sincere thanks for sharing his passion and literary talents in completing what we think is a *Henkaline Memories* Masterpiece. What began as his personal chronicle was unselfishly extended to each of us, in order to express our own personal memories. But be warned, in a few places through the pages, the recollections have been greatly embellished especially for the entertainment of our children and to put a smile on your face. Thanks again Jack, for sharing and taking the helm of our adventures! It has been a wonderful trip. Without you, it would still be on the cutting board.

Anita Pearson and Char Henkaline

Your hours of reading and editing our stories, correcting grammar, editing the flow of events and helping make our stories come to life is very much appreciated. You both have put the final touches to help make this book what it is today.

Keith Pearson

Your publishing talents are very much appreciated. This book would only be in paper text if you would not have helped us complete our memoires' book.

Henkaline Family Members

As you read our pages, we would be pleased for you also, to take the opportunity to pass it on. May each member of your family receive the warmth of your memories.

Forward

The memories file began as a personal journal entry in my lap top computer as early as 1994 when I frequently traveled on business. I felt the need to make a record of my childhood for my family. The initial entries were short and offered just a small caption of some interesting events from my early days. The few pages of data were collected over a few months and laid dormant for approximately fourteen years. During this time a friend named Tim Giffin died instantly while jogging. He was young and a wonderful teacher in our school district. He was loved by all his students and his death was a shock to the community. He left behind a beautiful wife and three children. After his funeral we learned from his wife Kathy that Tim was faithful to record a daily journal. Kathy went on to explain how much Tim's journal meant to her and their children. Her message inspired me to return to my memory file and add more stories. I realized that I did not know anything about my Mother's and Dad's childhood days and I wanted my wife Sharon, my son Chris, his wife Laura, and my grandchildren, to have the opportunity to hear some of the interesting and fun times I experienced while growing up. In 2008 I dedicated my lunch period at work to pick up where I left off in my memory's data base.

I found that as I entered my stories, I began to remember other great times I had with my parents and my siblings. It became a fun activity and it was then that I realized what a wonderful childhood I had and how much love we had in our family. As the stories entries began to mount, I began to understand that I was recording something very special about my family. I mentioned my story's to my sister, Anita, and she asked to see a copy. After receiving my memories she told me the stories were great and asked if she could add her stories to the list to share with her family. I was excited by her interest and stated the memories should become a Henkaline family collection. I then asked my older brother, Jerry, to get involved and he began to enter his stories. My younger brother, Ken, finally became engaged and we were on our way to the Henkaline kids compiling memories for this book.

There have been many revisions of our memories to provide the book that you see. The genealogy portion was provided by members of the John Henkaline family. Pictures have been collected from all the Henkaline kids and placed in select areas to better tell our stories. Many hours of editing, correcting and organizing has been offered by Anita and Char Henkaline and publishing has been made possible by Anita's eldest son, Keith Pearson. It is important to note that none of these memories could have been possible without the love, dedication and care from our wonderful Mother and Dad. In our stories we call our Dad different names. I remember call him Daddy until I grew up. My brothers and sister sometimes called him Pops, Popsy or just Dad. In any case his name was given with respect to a man that we all loved dearly.

What you are about to read has the power to create pleasant memories, a feeling of safety with family, and a look back at the stories that made each resident an individual and all a family. The time period takes you from the childhood memories that began on Hathaway Road and continues on into our adult lives. Though there have been a few tears, we are pleased to tell you about our childhood home and its magic to form pleasant memories and thoughts. Whenever past moments have time to creep back into our minds, the magic shows itself every time. We have waited until now, as adults, for our memories to reflect on our lives.

Jack B. Henkaline

CONTENTS

Chapter 4 - Jack Blaine Henkaline

Chapter 8 – A Special Memorial To Missie

Chapter 9 - Final Reflections

INTRODUCTION

The Memories in this book are dedicated to our parents with much love and respect. This book is presented to all the extended Henkaline Family for their enlightenment and understanding of our family adventures.

The William H. and Olive O. Henkaline Family
Our family is rooted in a Creator who is infinitely and eternally greater than His creation. "As the days of a tree, so shall be the days of My people". Isaiah 65: 22.

God's work of creating is done; our work of praising Him has only begun.

William Henry Henkaline
Born August 18, 1906
Died August 25, 1983 at 77 years old
Olive Opal (Hittle) Henkaline
Born December 14, 1909
Died April 18, 1984 at 75 years old
Daughter
Anita Louise Henkaline Pearson
Born January 14, 1938
Daughter
Joyce Ann Henkaline
Born September 23, 1943
Died October 24, 1943 at one month and one day
Son
Jerry Wayne Henkaline
Born August 15, 1945
Son
Jack Blaine Henkaline
Born August 18, 1947
Son
Kenneth Gene Henkaline
Born January 12, 1949

Mother As A Young Girl

We don't know when or where this picture was taken. It appears she was all dressed up to go to a special event.

Olive Opal Henkaline

Daddy In California

We think this picture was taken when Daddy was visiting Uncle Wayne in California. The time period was probably before he married our Mother.

Music - - -	Orchestra
Chorus - - - -	Class
Invocation - - - -	Rev. Clark Dennison
Piano Solo - - -	Mabel E. Bateman
Class History - - - -	Marie Zeck
Violin Solo - - - -	George Holzapfel
Valedictory - - - -	Richard P. Applegate
Solo - - - -	John Lloyd Keltner
Piano Solo - - - -	Mary J. Brooks
Class Address - - - -	D. C. Ward
Violin Duett - -	Mrs. Mary Mangas, Roy E. Shierling
Presenting of Diplomas - -	W. A. Brooks
Response - - -	County Supt. Chas. A. Wilt
Quartette - -	Velma Strait, Mary L. Hufford, Gladys L. Minnich, Gladys P. Boggs
Benediction - - -	Rev. Clark Dennison
Music - - - -	Orchestra

Exercises of Commencement

Jackson Township Centralized High School

on the evening of Friday May the Seventh

at eight o'clock

High School Auditorium

Baccalaureate Sermon Sunday afternoon at two-thirty,
May the second, by Reverend Zimmerman

William Henry Henkaline High School
Graduation Exercises and Commencement

Mother And Dad - The early years

We don't have a lot of details about how our parents met. We know they both lived in Dayton, Ohio. We think Fern Henkaline, a cousin to our mother and married to our Uncle Stanley, was the person who introduced them.

Olive Opal Henkaline

William Henry Henkaline

Reverend Milton Wiseley - Married Mother and Daddy On November 29, 1935

Bill Henkaline In Uniform

Bill And Olive Henkaline

Daddy Working At The Gas Station

Mother and Daddy In Their Early Years

One of Dad's early professional jobs was managing a gas station in Dayton, Ohio. We think this is the job he held when he was introduced to Mother.

Our Daddy During Early Days Of Marriage

CHAPTER 1

Road Sign To Our House (Picture Taken 2011)

1. The Henkaline Kids' Memories

There was a house located on Hathaway Road, outside of Woodington, Ohio, that was our childhood home. The house was built in 1900 and featured 1610 sq. ft. of living space. The large barn close to the house was later built in 1901. When you drove by, it looked like a very ordinary farm with a two story white house, a big white barn and some out buildings. There was a short driveway from the road with a slight incline that led to a parking area in front of the barn. The house and buildings were well kept and made us proud to call this our home. Our family felt safe and comfortable in this house and we have some very pleasant memories we want to share from our experiences.

An enclosed back porch was the first room you entered into the rear portion of the house. This room opened to a plain, but large, kitchen. The kitchen was where our mother prepared some great meals. We remember a table standing Kitchen Aid mixer that was equipped with a large stainless steel bowl. Mother would fill that bowl with mashed potatoes for almost every evening meal. We saw the serving plates piled with meat and fresh vegetables. Our dessert was some of the best fruit pies your mouth could ever taste. The kitchen was a great place to visit when you felt a need to grab a snack between meals because there was always food left over from previous meals. When your sweet tooth kicked in, you could always find a gallon container of ice cream in the refrigerator freezer and a can of Hershey's chocolate in the cabinet.

Our kitchen served as a multiple function room such as a place to get away from the crowd or a room to study for school homework. We had a gray metal table with chrome trim and padded vinyl yellow and gray chairs that made the room comfortable to relax. In the winter months the kitchen was the warmest room in the house. Another kitchen event was when our dad rounded up the boys, one at a time, and made them sit on an adult high chair to give a bi-weekly hair cut. Our dad's haircutting seemed to stop time in space and the event gave the boys a real opportunity to carefully study every detail of the room and ceiling.

Our living room was a special gathering place for our family in the evening. It was a huge room which accommodated the entire family. The light mint green walls and dark natural woodwork gave this room character and created a pleasant place to rest or watch our black and white television. The living room furniture consisted of a long low backed sofa, a green swivel rocker, a wooden rocker and a tan recliner. The sofa ends were angled slightly upward and positioned just above the sitting surface. This feature allowed us to lie on the couch and use the sofa ends as a pillow to watch TV. The floor became the overflow for any of the boys not lucky enough to claim a chair. Each night when our Dad entered the living room from a hard days work it was a ritual that if any of the kids were sitting in the tan recliner they would automatically get up and give Dad his chair. We don't ever remember our dad demanding this chair, but we just knew he was tired and it was his chair. Mother usually would sit in the rocking chair.

The House Where We Grew Up

The front door of our house was never used by family members or friends of the family. The back door to the enclosed porch was closest to the driveway parking area and the most convenient way to enter the house. Only strangers who came to our house would knock on the front door.

The Hathaway House In 2011

Picture Taken Of The Hathaway House In 2011
New Siding, New Roof, New Windows And A New Front Porch Has Been Added

Picture Taken Of The Hathaway House In 2011

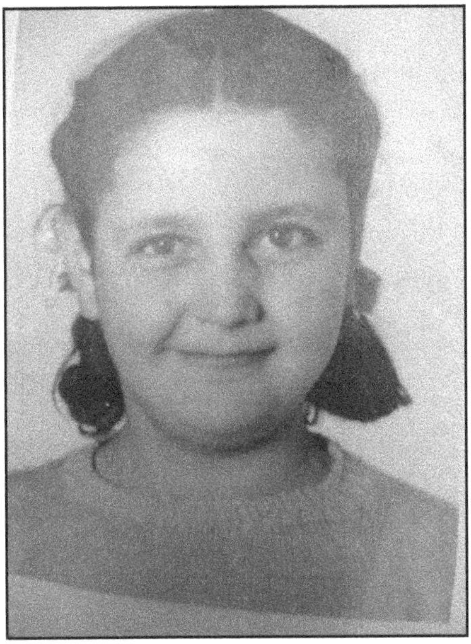

Anita Louise Henkaline

Jerry Wayne Henkaline

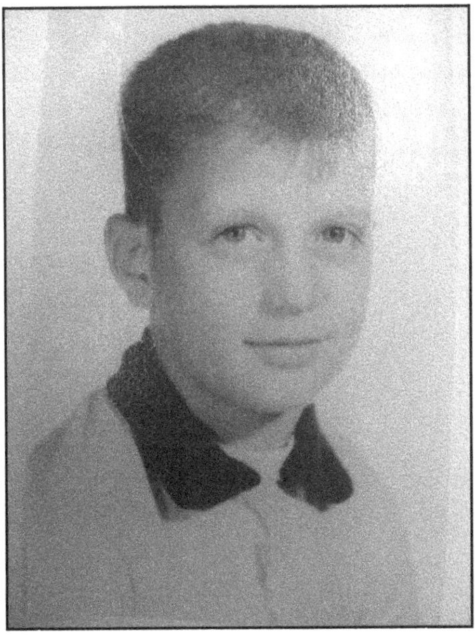

Jack Blaine Henkaline

Kenneth Gene Henkaline

OUR MEMORIES

CHAPTER 2

Anita Louise Henkaline

2. Our Sister Joyce Ann

It would have been so nice to have our sister, Joyce Ann, alive and well and in the middle of all the shenanigans. We would have been a great team! She would have helped me to help our parents keep our brothers on the straight and narrow!

INFANT GIRL DIES OF WHOOPING COUGH

Darke County Farm Couple Mourn Loss of Baby Daughter

Mr. and Mrs. William Henkaline, residing four miles southwest of Ansonia, are mourning the death of their four-week old daughter, Joyce Ann, which occurred yesterday. Death was attributed to whooping cough.

Besides the father and mother, one sister, Anita, and two grandmothers, Mrs. Sadie Hittle and Mrs. Pearl Summers, both of Ansonia R. R., survive.

Funeral services will be held at two p. m. Tuesday at the Fisher-Becker funeral home in Ansonia. The Rev. Richard Norris will officiate. Burial will be in Ansonia cemetery.

Joyce Ann Henkaline died one month and one day from birth, losing her fight with whooping cough. During that time our parents lived in a country home on Winrick Pike, where I was born in 1938 and lived until I was about 5 years old. It was hard for me to understand at that age why my beautiful little sister had to leave us. Not until we became involved in church and I learned The Plan of Salvation, God's Grace and Eternal Life, did I finally understand that she's waiting for us in Heaven ... along with Popsy, Mother, Missie, and other family members, who joined her later.

3. The Move To The Farm

I have such fond memories of our home on Hathaway Road. It had great farm acreage and lots of yard for me to mow. There was a fish pond, wonderful beds of my favorite iris, tiger lilies and lily-of-the-valley flowers (to name a few) and a multitude of other plants and trees. There was a plum orchard and room for a nice vegetable garden, which allowed our food freezer to be filled with the veggies, along with abundant portions of meats, to be enjoyed throughout the year. Mother and Popsy were hard workers and always supplied our needs.

Anita - A Pretty Little Girl With Her Dolly

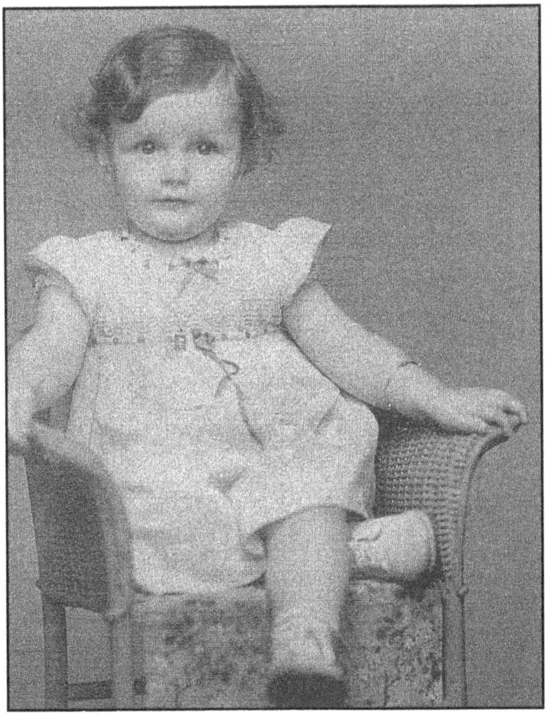

Anita In Her Hollywood Pose

4. Trouble

Before the brothers were born, I was given the sweetest little dog named Trouble. He was anything but trouble! He was given to me by the Ansonia Methodist Minister and his family. Maybe somehow they knew I'd be inheriting "moments of trouble" when the brothers came along! My dog was the beginning of my love for pets. Another favorite that crossed my path was a bunny rabbit. I was never told what happened to that little fuzz-ball, but I think I remember having a nice stew dinner shortly after his disappearance! I'd rather not think about that anymore. Instead, I'd rather remember the shiny tricycle Uncle Henry and Aunt Della gave me as a consolation gift.

Daddy – Mother – Anita With Her Dog Trouble

5. Beginning School At Woodington

My education began in 1944, at a nearby two-room schoolhouse in Woodington, Ohio. Classes were from First to Sixth Grade. One room was our class room. The other was used for storage and indoor adventures. I have fond memories of my first grade teacher, Mrs. Bateman and all the special activities she prepared for her students. She was the greatest! Then there was my school bus driver who was an interesting man named

Isem Cox. He was a bit scary to me because of his crippled body. With time I sensed his good qualities and discovered he was a nice person. He faithfully picked us up and delivered us each school day in his personal car. He even installed a special handle to grab helping us to enter the car and take our seats.

The Woodington School House (Picture Taken 2011)

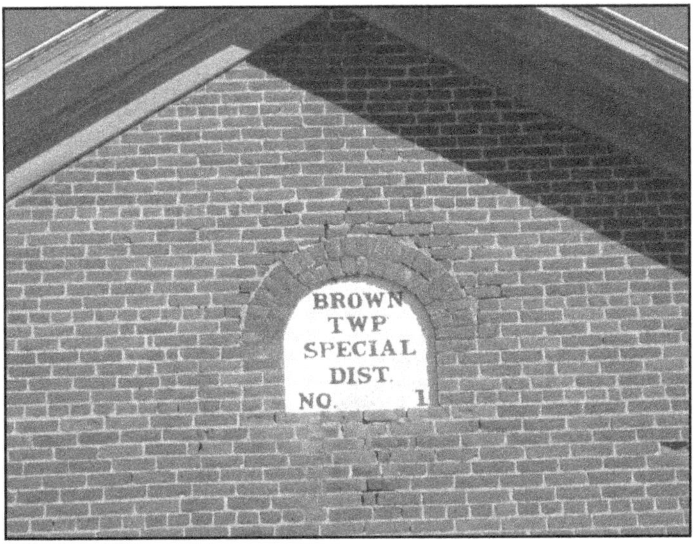

Plaque Identification Of School House

6. Woodington, Ohio

In this small town of a few hundred residents was a historical claim to fame of the well-known resident, Annie Oakley, the famous sharpshooter and later, Lowell Thomas, a prominent national newscaster, Hall of Fame recipient and famous American Literature Journalist. They both have since been honored with a museum in their names in nearby Greenville, Ohio.

Anita With Jerry On Hathaway Road

7. Changing Schools

At the beginning of my fourth grade year, my parents were encouraged to make a school zoning change to be in the Ansonia School District in order for me to receive a more solid education. Unfortunately, my first experience there turned out to be most difficult! My teacher always made me think she had horns under her hair because she was so mean, especially when it was time to study arithmetic! (I'll protect the guilty by not naming her!)

After that year, my school days were a whole lot more enjoyable; other than that occasion "down by the bridge, at the north end of Hathaway Road:

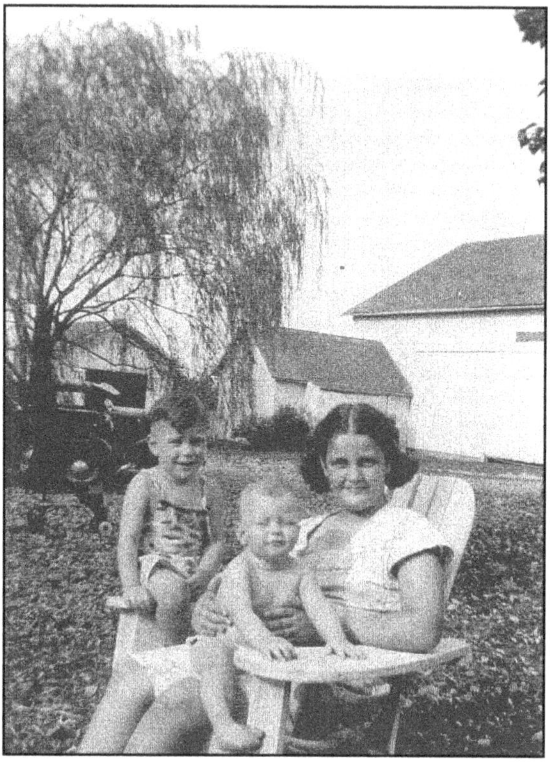

Anita With Jerry And Jack On Her Lap On Hathaway Road

8. The X-Posure

Until the school zoning paperwork was completed, I was not eligible to ride the Ansonia school bus making it necessary to find other transportation for a short while. The Folks were pleased to connect with the Woodington Congregational Church pastor's wife who was a teacher at the school. They made a plan for me to walk to the end of the road where she would pick me up at a designated time. It all worked well until one day my wait for her was too long! A car stopped just before crossing the bridge near the roadside where I was standing. A man got out of his car and invited me to come to him. Because he wasn't pleased that I declined his invitation he decided to expose himself and started walking toward me. Thank God, Mrs. Clevenger came just in time causing him to have to move his car in order for her to cross over the bridge. I remember being scared out of my wits, but I didn't let her know anything was wrong. When I arrived in my classroom, I fell apart emotionally and my teacher asked what was wrong. A short time later she sent me to the principal's office where I was introduced to the County Sheriff. He asked me to describe what had happened. Of course, my parents were notified and together a plan was set for the next day. My Dad would be hiding under the bridge just in case the man came again. I would have nothing to do with that plan because I was too afraid. Thankfully, they recognized my fear and the decision was made for me to sit in the car with Popsy at the spot where I usually waited and if the man returned I was to let him know. About the same time as the day before, the man had the nerve to show up again. This time he had a long wagon attached to his car. When he noticed us sitting in the car he decided he'd better move on. It didn't take Popsy long to put the pedal to the metal; never letting him out of our sight. The increased speed of the man's vehicle and attached wagon caused it to sway that became uncontrollable and impossible to stay on the road. To keep from having an accident it was necessary for him to stop. Immediately, Popsy got out of his car and stormed up to confront the driver who by this time was locking his doors and rolling up his window.

We were shocked to discover the pervert was Amish. Understanding that because he didn't touch me, legal charges couldn't be made. Popsy followed the Sheriff's directions to "scare the 'hell' out of him" and give serious threats, telling him his name was on their list and his actions would be watched from that day forward! Mission accomplished, but it took a long time for me to feel safe again.

Daddy Anita And Mother

9. Plain And Simple Entertainment

Since I was raised as an only child for seven years until my first brother, Jerry, arrived, it was necessary to use my imagination to be entertained. The most favorite time was playing with my doll house that had furniture for every room. Mother's spools of thread were my pretend people. Truthfully, it was hard to give that doll house away for my cousin Ann to enjoy. In the spring I loved playing in the cornfield until residue from the fresh corn stock tassels fell on the back of my neck and caused a rash. That ended that game. Next came the woods where I discovered arrow heads. Where are they now? One of my favorite treats was receiving a comic book that I'd ask Mother to buy when she went to town to grocery shop. It was better than candy!

Anita In Her Sunday Clothes

10. Earning My Keep

It wasn't always fun and games. Helping Mother do chores kept me busy with lots of different duties. When it was dishwashing time she could never understand why at that precise moment I felt the need to go to the bathroom. I told her they were 'dishwater pains'. The meals that created those dishwashing tasks were always delicious. I remember best, Mother's scrumptious pies. We'll always remember when Popsy asked her to make a grape pie. In our world, we had never heard of grape pie, but Mother created a prize!

It was always my duty to set the dining room table before guests arrived for a meal. Those china dishes were beautiful, as well as the pretty clear pink drinking glasses. Of course, our everyday meals were served in the kitchen. It was a good thing! Popsy always threatened to wear a raincoat to the table because sitting next to the boys would always get messy. They never failed to spill something, especially glasses of milk.

11. Steam Heat

The light green hue that complimented our living and dining room walls that the brothers remember so well was not always there. I know they will be impressed to learn that I was given the task to help remove several layers of wallpaper from those walls with a steamer before they were so beautifully painted.

12. My Bedroom

I always loved my first-floor bedroom ... being able to sneak in from a date and no one ever hearing me, NOT! Later I learned that being a parent develops wide-open eyes and keen ears to not miss a beat of the comings-and-goings of our kidlets! But I digress! Behind the curtained French doors by the living room, my bedroom was furnished with a dresser, a bed, and a chest of drawers. The only place to hang my clothes in the room was a coat rack. I was pleased to be assigned a nice sized attic space behind the upstairs bathroom as my closet.

There was only one scary night in that room that I can remember, when it seemed there was someone outside my window looking in. No doubt it was the cedar branches rubbing against the window, with the help of the wind, but it caused a sleepless night on Hathaway Road!

13. My Version Of The Dating Game

The brothers always found it necessary to check out 'The Victim' before and after each date. They loved to grade him and didn't miss an opportunity to act like The Three Stooges behind his back while he was meeting my parents! The fellows I dated after moving from home didn't know how fortunate they were to not face my brothers' scrutiny.

Grandmother Sarah Hittle

14. Grandmother Sarah (Sadie) Hittle

From time to time Grandmother would come to stay with us after Grandfather Hittle passed away. It was fun to sit next to her and listen to her sing folk songs and tell fun stories as she sat in the rocking chair in our living room. She loved harvesting honey from her bee hives. The special garb she wore for that occasion was most intriguing. Not one inch of her body was exposed, but the big hat with a screen front was the best. She also loved to use our churn to make delicious butter. The chore was always accomplished on our closed-in back porch just outside our kitchen

We never had the joy of knowing Grandfather Henry Hittle. I was told he was blind and made brooms as his livelihood. He and Grandmother shared their Christian faith and musical talents on a regular basis in their community.

Grandmother Sadie Hittle

Grandfather Henry Hittle

Their eight children: Uncle Ed (Nellie), Uncle Talmage (Emma), Uncle Earl (Vergie), Aunt Carrie (Ira), Aunt Ethel (Muncie), Aunt Della (Henry), Uncle Francis (Mary) and our mother, Olive (William), honored their heritage and love of family.

Great Grandfather Hittle

Our Uncle's and Aunt's From The Hittle Family
Back Row - Uncle Henry Buser– Mother – Aunt Vergie and Uncle Earl Hittle
Front Row - Aunt Carrie Gibson – Aunt Mary Hittle– Aunt Ethel Marshall – Aunt Della Buser

15. Grandfather John Henry and Grandmother Pearl Henkaline

Reflections of the one I've been told I resemble, are impressionable, but with questions. Because we failed to ask when we were younger, in 2010 we connected with our cousin Keven, who has shared his recollections of Grandfather John Henry Henkaline, whom we never met. Quoting Keven, "He was a kind, six foot tall, handsomely thin gentleman with a neatly trimmed mustache". He and Grandmother ended their marriage sometime in the late 20's or early 30's, but not before having their five children: Aunt Nellie (Charlie Shiverdecker), Uncle Stanley Fern (Hittle), our dad, William (Olive Hittle), John (Marian McKay) and Uncle Wayne (Gertrude Ann Coats). Uncle Wayne was the only sibling still at home at the time of their parting.

It was thought that Grandpa wanted more adventure and more money, rather than living on a 20 acre plot of land outside of Ansonia. He went to Dayton, Ohio and found work operating rides at Lakeside Amusement Park. He later worked as a bartender at Doc's Corner Family Tavern. He was called 'Doc' and lived in an apartment on the premises. He also would sometimes take care of the owner's children. Cousins Keven and Bob would occasionally stop in at Doc's Corner on their way home from grammar school and receive a candy bar from Grandpa.

Grandmother Pearl (Henkaline) Foreman - Summers

16. Remembering Grandmother Henkaline

Grandmother was remembered to be ambitious and always quite independent. She started her family at age eighteen, while Grandfather was 26. Uncle Wayne said Grandmother was quite adamant for some reason about the spelling of her maiden name: Foreman (which I believe she changed back from Henkaline to Foreman to Summers). There is rumor that her father or grandfather was an Indian who had been adopted, but his Indian name or tribe has never been verified.

Grandmother got tired of asking the neighbors to bring her things from town so she bought a car and taught herself how to drive out in a field. After the purchase, the local law enforcement officer told her on one of her many trips to town that he was going to take the car away if she didn't get a driver's license and a license plate. With or without ... she managed to make it to our house on many occasions. After her divorce, it was told that a man named Summers stopped at her house looking for a hand out. He had a driver's license and they got married. We don't know what happened to Mr. Sommers or anything about their marriage.

Grandmother continued to drive after their marriage. One time she'd made an 'impression' on the front side of our barn because she confused the gas pedal and the brake! I always wondered when Grandmother died, if her habit of eating lard sandwiches had anything to do with her demise.

Grandmother Henkaline's Homestead

17. Grandmother Henkaline's Musical Talents

After Grandmother passed away, we learned that she had some musical talent. The song "My New Love" is an example of what she wrote and applied for copyright records.

MY NEW LOVE
Words by PEARL SOMMERS
Music by PEARL SOMMERS
I once was hap-py, light-heart-ed and gay, I knew no sor-row nor care. I
Those words so cru-el were so hard to bear, My heart was bro-ken with grief. I
loved a boy who I thot loved me too, Our plea-sure and joy we would share. We
longed for some-one to heal the pain, But found no source of re- - lief. Then
spent hap-py hours to - geth - er, We talked of love so true. Un-
one sad day as I wan - dered, I found a friend so true. He
-til one day I re - ceive. a note, That said I no long-er love you. The
was so gen-tle both man-ly and brave, He said my dear I love you.
Copyright 1948-BY-PEARL SOMMERS

Chorus
lines of wor - ry have all left my face, I feel so hap - py and
free. I know my new love can take his place, He's proved it so clear-ly to
me. He healed a heart that was bro-ken, He took a - way the
pain. The words he speaks are so ten- der to me, He's
made me hap - py a - - gain. The - gain.
MY NEW LOVE-2

CERTIFICATE OF REGISTRATION OF CLAIM TO COPYRIGHT IN A MUSICAL COMPOSITION

Registration No. ©CL unpub. 112329 | Class E

This Is To Certify that the following statements for the musical composition herein named have been made a part of the records of the Copyright Office. In witness whereof the seal of the Copyright Office is hereto affixed.

Sam B. Warner
Register of Copyrights
United States of America

NOT VALID WITHOUT COPYRIGHT OFFICE IMPRESSION SEAL

1. Copyright Owner or Owners (Give full names and addresses)
Pearl Sommers, (Pseu for) Pearl May Sommers Route 2 Versailles, Ohio.

2. Title of Musical Composition MY NEW LOVE

3. Composers, Authors, Etc. After "Nature of authorship" insert, for example: music, words, translation, arrangement, compilation, or other suitable description. Full name (including full middle name), pseudonym (if any), and year of birth and, if dead, year of death, are requested for cataloging purposes.

(a) Name Pearl Sommers, (Pseu for) Pearl (First) May (Middle) Sommers (Last) Citizenship U.S.A. (Country)
Nature of authorship Words and Music Birth 1886 (Year) Death (Year)
Domicile U.S.A. (Address)

(b) Name (First) (Middle) (Last) Citizenship (Country)
Nature of authorship Birth (Year) Death (Year)
Domicile (Address)

(c) Name (First) (Middle) (Last) Citizenship (Country)
Nature of authorship Birth (Year) Death (Year)
Domicile (Address)

(d) Name (First) (Middle) (Last) Citizenship (Country)
Nature of authorship Birth (Year) Death (Year)
Domicile (Address)

4. FOR PUBLISHED WORKS ONLY. Give date when copies bearing copyright notice were first placed on sale, sold, or publicly distributed (Month, day, and year)

Send Certificate, Refund (If Any), and Other Communications to:

Name Pearl Sommers
Address Route 2 (Number and Street)
Versailles, (City) (Zone) Ohio. (State)

DATE OF RECEIPT IN COPYRIGHT OFFICE
APPLICATION JAN 14 1948
ONE COPY OF MUSICAL COMPOSITION JAN 14 1948
TWO COPIES OF MUSICAL COMPOSITION

Grandmother Henkaline's Music Certificate of Registration

18. Grandmother Henkaline's Painting

We learned that Grandmother also liked to paint. The painting below is on a wooden base. What is interesting is that it has livestock and their breed listed on the back of the base. The date on the bottom is August 27, 1947. Although the painting will not make the art gallery in New York City we are proud to say it was painted by our Grandmother.

19. Music, Music, Music

After trying to learn to play the piano and a school purchased saxophone, I chose to go vocal. It was always an honor to be invited to sing for various occasions; in school, in church, for weddings and private parties. Popsy was instrumental in getting me invited to sing at the big Hobart Christmas Party. (I hope I made him proud!)

Left To Right - Daddy – Irene Drake – Anita
Picture Taken At The Hobart Christmas Party

20. Uncle Francis Hittle's And His Musical Talents

Uncle Francis also had exceptional musical talents. He sang in Christian men quartets and traveled around the area to local churches. He had the ability to sing all four parts of a musical arrangement. He provided this talent by purchasing two tape recorders and using them to produce a one man choir. First he would sing bass on one recorder. Then he would play his bass voice back on the first recorder and sing along as another bass while recording both voices on recorder number two. He did this over and over until he has a complete bass section recorded. Next he took his full base section and sang as a tenor. The same technique with the tenor voice provided the men's portion of the arrangement. His next challenge was to do the same thing with the alto and soprano parts. When complete he had a recording which sounded like an entire choir, by using only his voice. An unsuspecting listener would never know it was a one man choir.

21. Remembering The Results Of The Recession

There were gas coupons as well as rations on sugar and flour during the recession. I always had the duty of putting a red colored tablet inside the 'butter' bag to make it yellow. It was intriguing to watch Mother carefully use the milk separator, watching the cream come to the top of the container. How did it do that?

Popsy and Mother became real scholars of thrift as they survived the recession. Due to these times of shortages, their wisdom followed through for years to come. They never caused us to feel underprivileged, but taught us to be thankful for what we had.

I also remember a time or two when everyone had to turn off all our lights and pull the drapes at nighttime not just in the larger towns, but also in the countryside where we lived. I don't know if the folks were given a schedule or if word was passed from community to community, but the purpose of the exercise was due to a fear of enemy bombing during the current World War II.

The Henkaline Family In The Late 1950's

22. General Comments Made In The Year 1955!

"I'll tell you one thing, if things keep going the way they are, it's going to be impossible to buy a weeks groceries for $10.00."

"Have you seen the new cars coming out next year? It won't be long before $1,000.00 will only buy a used one."

"If cigarettes keep going up in price, I'm going to quit! 20 cents a pack is ridiculous."

"Did you hear the post office is thinking about charging 7 cents just to mail a letter?"

"If they raise the minimum wage to $1.00, nobody will be able to hire outside help at the store."

"When I first started driving, who would have thought gas would someday cost 25 cents a gallon. Guess we'd be better off leaving the car in the garage."

"I'm afraid to send my kids to the movies any more. Ever since they let Clark Gable get by with saying *'DAMN'* in GONE WITH THE WIND, it seems every new movie has either HELL or DAMN in it."

"I read the other day where some scientist thinks it's possible to put a man on the moon by the end of the century. They even have some fellows they call astronauts preparing for it down in Texas."

"Did you see where some baseball player just signed a contract for $50,000 a year just to play ball? It wouldn't surprise me if someday they'll be making more than the President."

"I never thought I'd see the day all our kitchen appliances would be electric. They are even making electric typewriters now."

"It's too bad things are so tough nowadays. I see where a few married women are having to work to make ends meet."

"It won't be long before young couples are going to have to hire someone to watch their kids so they can both work."

"I'm afraid the Volkswagen car is going to open the door to a whole lot of foreign business."

"Thank goodness I won't live to see the day when the government takes half our income in taxes. I sometimes wonder if we are electing the best people to government."

"The drive-in restaurant is convenient in nice weather, but I seriously doubt they will ever catch on."

"There is no sense going on short trips anymore for a weekend. It costs nearly $2.00 a night to stay in a hotel."

"No one can afford to be sick anymore. At $15.00 a day in the hospital, it's too rich for my blood."

"If they think I'll pay 30 cents for a hair cut, forget it."

23. Mother's Feed Sack Dress Creations

Someone had the great idea of making grain sacks with a nice soft cloth and colorful flowers on them. Mother made numerous trips to the nearby Woodington Elevator to 'kill two birds with one stone' purchasing feed grain for our animals and then being careful to select the prettiest prints to sew outfits for both of us. I always felt real special wearing my new dresses!

Mother and Daddy In Our Growing Up Years

24. Graduating From Ansonia High School....Affectionately Coined 'Ansumonia Tech' By The Brothers.

Of course, like many, my senior year (1956) was the most fun! It was filled with music, exercising my acting ability in our junior and senior class plays, yearbook activities, local school field trips and at the end of the year, the BIG Excursion to New York City and Washington, D.C.

25. Jerry And His Sports Talents

One of the secrets that few people know about our brother Jerry is the fact that because of his talented sports abilities, his high school coach encouraged him to further his education in order to become a certified educator and coach. Jerry's coach told him that he had the ability and personality to be a great coach and teach others his skills.

Anita - All Grown Up

26. My Employment Experiences

Between my Junior and Senior High School Years (1955-56) I was hired at the Darke County Home in Greenville, Ohio, as a 'Cinderella' scrubbing long hallway floors on my knees, serving meals to staff in their dining room and looking for my prince.

27. My First Job At The Bank

My first bank position, located in my hometown, prepared me to meet and serve people and be responsible for the challenge of balancing my records and duties each day. I took those beginning work experiences and allowed them to mature and enhance my future.

28. Now Away From Home

One of my most unique jobs was at the Satellite Bank in Florida, where I worked in public relations and served as an unofficial 'Welcome Wagon Lady' visiting new residents in the area and giving them brochures of our bank services. This was also the bank where we had a visit by what was described by a bank officer as a few members of the Miami Mafia. I didn't stick around to find out the nature of their business. Call me a 'weenie' if you wish, but I hid in a nearby closet until they were gone.

Another memorable experience was working in a suburban bank just outside of St. Paul, Minnesota. I was first assigned to a desk in the loan department. It wasn't the most enjoyable assignment I'd ever had and I was glad when my bank officer boss asked if I'd move to the receptionist/ courtesy desk to fill the vacancy of that position.

The best I can figure somewhere along the line, I innocently placed a loan document in the hands of someone who took issue with the recorded information.

It seemed to be a regular winter workday near the Christmas holidays, but strangely on that morning, I was given orders not to permit anyone to interrupt the president or allow anyone to go into his office. Sure enough, it didn't take long before two well dressed gentlemen were in front of my desk making the forbidden request. I did my best to refer them to another bank officer, but when they flashed their official government badges they expected me to usher them into what I later discovered would become the 'doom-tomb'.

By days end, the president managed to come by my desk and addressed me with a few choice words! All I could manage to say to him was, "Well, Merry Christmas To You Too!" Other bank officers apologized for his rudeness, and it didn't take long to discover what actually happened behind those closed doors. The results of that loan document managed to reserve him a cot and free meals behind bars for awhile!

29. Anita Pearson Among Five Candidates For Military "Wife Of The Year" Award

MRS. PEARSON ... Candidate

Greenville Daily Advocate Newspaper Article
A former Darke County resident, Mrs. Wallace K. Pearson, daughter of Mr. and Mrs. W.H. Henkaline, Greenville, has been selected to represent her husband's respective unit at Griffiss Air Force Base, Rome, New York, as a nominee in the Sixth Annual Military Wife of the Year Contest for 1972. Mrs. Pearson is among five candidates who hopes to become "Wife of the Year." She is a graduate of Ansonia High School and wife of the Chaplain (Capt.) Wallace Pearson, of the 416th Combat Support Group and Family Services. Mrs. Pearson has served as a church receptionist as well as a secretary for a college professor, a college vice president and an academic dean in St. Paul, Minn. She has many hobbies including reading, sports, travel and sightseeing, listening to people and choral work for radio and television. Mrs. Pearson also is a Red Cross volunteer, a "Mustard Seed" (drug abuse) program volunteer and is on the staff of the Big Brother Griffiss Program. Mrs. Pearson spends much time with the Big Brother Program and enjoys this work very much. This program provides guidance and companionship to youngsters whose own fathers are serving remote tours or are missing in action or prisoners of war. She says her most gratifying project is bringing cheer to the old folks at the Oneida County Hospital. According to her mother, Mrs. Henkaline, Anita says, "It doesn't cost money to give a

smile, a listening ear, or to share delight and pleasure for a completed handcrafted article. I've also had the delight of singing for them and their tears of appreciations were the best thanks I could ever receive." This is a special honor for Mrs. Pearson and I hope to hear when she becomes "Military Wife of the Year" at Rome. I'm sure Mrs. Henkaline will keep me informed of the progress of the contest. For the record, a lovely friend earned the honor—well deserved!

30. Blessings

Thinking back on all my years, I must admit there were some interesting circumstances that crossed my path, but none were richer than my family ties. I've expressed my love and appreciation in remembrance of my parents, and now, I thank my brothers for all they mean to me. They have accepted my Pearson Family with open arms and great respect.

Jerry's open and generous heart makes us feel so welcome in his home, allowing us to kick back, relax and visit quietly. He arranges hometown treats and trips to old stomping grounds. He's always ready and willing to pick us up and deliver us at the airport on our every visit. How priceless!

Jack is known affectionately as our Family Activities Director, arranging fun things for us to do and Sharon compliments him by making us feel like we're in a First-Class Bed and Breakfast (Lunch and Dinner) in their home. What A Treat!

Ken and Julie have a most cozy and wonderful upstairs suite for our pleasure. We've made a tradition of eating at our favorite Mexican restaurant and topping off the evening with a delicious Winan's special flavored coffee. Can't beat it!

Gratefully, I've been honored, with the brothers' blessing to receive Mother's beautiful necklace that she purchased on her trip to the Holy Land. I wear it with a great deal of love!

The Pearson Family On Anita and Wally's Wedding Day
Kenneth – Keith – Anita – Wally - Beverly

31. 100 Knoll Avenue In Greenville, 'O-H-I-O'

I found my prince (Wally Pearson) in 1968 and he gave me 'The Glass Slipper'. His military career allowed me to join him in many new adventures. This was the address where memories were started for the Pearson Clan. Our children, Keith and Kenneth, remember the deal they had with Grandfather always wanting to sit next to him at mealtime because he allowed them to slide their 'not so favorite' vegetables on his plate, while Grandmother was in the kitchen. It worked out for all three of them, because Grandfather enjoyed the likes of brussel sprouts and other green stuff; while the boys were able to proudly display their empty plates for Grandmother to see before she served dessert.

32. The Missing Tree

The Pearson boys are still sad about the missing tree in the front yard of Knoll Avenue they spent so much time climbing. It had to be removed to excavate the soil where tree roots surfaced and the ground was causing water draining problems. As we visit and cruise in front of this address now, it's like an empty hole in all of our hearts.

100 Knoll Avenue – Greenville, Ohio (Picture Taken 2011)

Pearson Family Picture

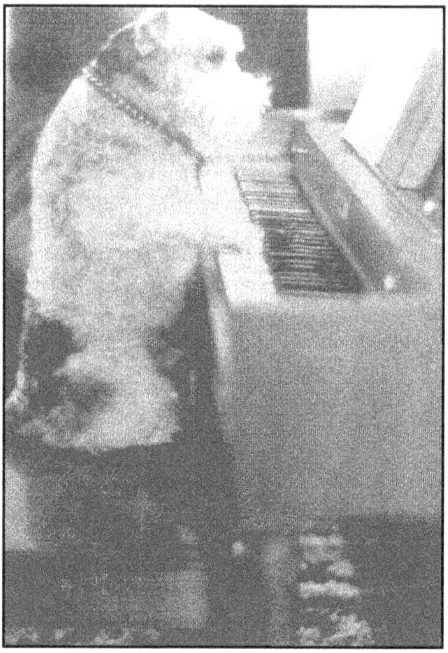

The Pearson Family Dog, Dusty, Who Inherited Anita's Musical Talents

33. Dollar Days In Greenville

It was Greenville's Dollar Day that sparked Beverly's desire to emulate Grandmother and her talent for finding the best bargains at this special yearly event. They would come home, display their purchases, calculate how much money they saved and then joke about how it was burning a hole in their pockets, wondering where and when to spend it.

Bev has carried the ability to find great savings into her adult life and proudly says, "Grandmother Henkaline would be proud of me!"

34. Pearson Family Visits To Knoll Avenue

Wally remembers his first warm August welcome, when there was no air-conditioning to comfort the sticky, humid days that are so common in the area at that time of year. The killer was even when The Folks had an air-conditioner installed later; it seemed to wait for his next visit to break down.

35. Wally Jobs On Knoll

Because Wally wanted to earn his "Favorite-Son-In-Law-In-The-Family" title, he found himself climbing up the TV antenna to make adjustments, changing water gaskets and helping Popsy with other important repairs. One of his rewards was getting to eat as many 'monster' tomatoes from Mother's vegetable garden as he could handle. He always enjoyed accompanying Pops while he ran his errands around town. It was first to the Shell Station to fill up the tank and then off to the bank and other miscellaneous errands. The favorite and most memorable time was getting to listen to him exercise his business savvy as he prepared to get the best offer at the Ford dealership. When he told them it was time for them to sharpen their pencil, they knew there wouldn't be a great profit when Bill Henkaline was finished making the deal.

The Henkaline Family In Front Of The Knoll Avenue Home

36. I'VE FOUND A TREASURE!

Recently, we found a cassette tape, dated September, 1981; with the voices of Mother and Popsy sharing family memories, along with details of their visit with us in Colorado Springs, Colorado.

After returning from Wally's tour of duty in Germany, we traveled to Greenville to visit The Folks and invited them to join us on our way to our next assignment at Peterson Air Force Base, CO. On the long trip back, Wally was scheduled to stop off and attend a conference in St. Louis for a couple of days; giving us the opportunity to heal any 'saddle sores' we may have acquired along the way. It was amusing to hear Popsy's comment more than once, that it seemed as though we'd never get out of Kansas! He sounded a lot like what we now hear from his son, Jerry's mouth when he travels more than across the street! (Obviously they've never traveled across Texas!)

We finally arrived at our new home on Silver Spur, and as usual, anticipated the arrival of the remainder of our household belongings, which included boxes of special purchases we'd made while traveling through Europe for three years. It was like watching children at Christmas as they helped us unpack our items. What fun it was to watch them share the joy and excitement of the task!

Conversations on the cassette tape include their knowledge of our Henkaline-Hittle ancestry, as well as their adventures together; beginning with their marriage on November 29th, 1935, and a list of all the places they had called home throughout their lives. My question and answer sessions included having Mother give 'show and tell' directions of how she prepared the crust for her delicious pies. Always so yummy! I also asked her to recite favorite poems Grandmother Hittle use to teach us, as well as folk songs she use to sing. But most of all, her talent of speaking 'Pig Latin' topped everything off in rare form. This is where we kind of lost control, laughing so hard. It was really a jolly good time!

It's true: Laughter is like good medicine.

It's going to be fun sharing all the memories on the tape with my Brothers, since they haven't heard our parent's voices since their 'graduation' to heaven: Popsy in 1983 and Mother in 1984.

For future family generations, I would like to suggest that YOU take the opportunity to record conversations with your loved ones, too. It's a real treasure you will cherish forever.

37. "Uncle Bud" Henkaline

Actually, his christened name was Clarence and he was a second cousin. He made it his duty to arrange his many visits to Mother and Pops, always at mealtime, and never knew when to leave. How many times have we mimicked Pops' reaction when he saw him coming: "Oh no, here comes B-U-D!" Over and over and over again, he'd repeat the goings on of his small world. Even the brothers received his visits and had to tolerate the stories of slopping the hogs and working at the cemetery. The most exciting episode was the discovery of marijuana growing in his cornfield. (Could it be that he sold 'a stash' or two, on the side, to add to his huge bank account?) But of course, I jest! At his death we learned that his inheritance was awarded to the Greenville Hospital. and the Greenville YMCA. We were glad to hear that Clarence's most generous contributions were given to a worthy cause.

38. The Head Of Our Family

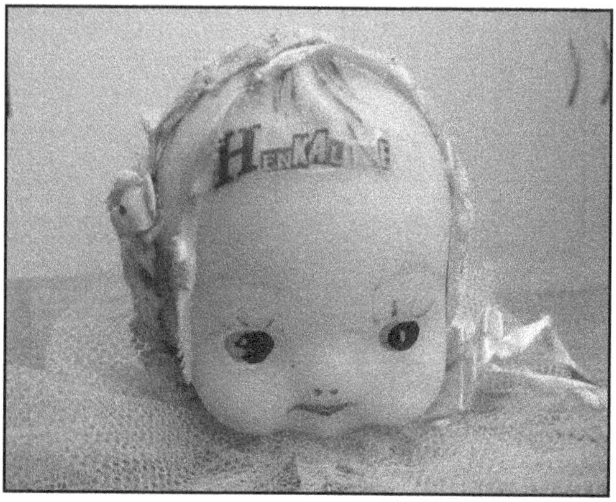

At our wedding reception, we were given the most unusual 'one-of-a-kind' wedding gift anyone could ever receive. It came in the form of a round wax candle, decorated with a painted kewpie-doll face, with lace and ribbon glued on top to represent a bonnet. Not knowing how or where to display it, we decided to share her with other family members in very special ways.

Mother and Popsy were the first recipients of our treasured gift. After a wonderful visit, they prepared packing their luggage for their trip home. At that time, we found a perfect opportunity to sneak in the bedroom and place our little 'gift' deep under their belongings; not to be discovered until they arrived at the end of their journey. From then on, it made its rounds to each by Brother and their families, and again to us at Air Force Bases around the world. At one of her return visits, we decided to dress her up a bit by placing letters on her forehead; christening her officially, 'The Henkaline Head'. She's had many interesting experiences along the way. One of which was earning her diploma at the college where I worked in California back in the 80's; studying at my desk every day. Now 40-plus years later, if she isn't placed in someone's luggage, she gets boxed in decorative gift wrapping to be given as a Christmas gift to an unsuspecting family member. With all the fun she created, it was only natural to add more surprise gifts to be given at future gatherings.

A new addition was added when Jack and Sharon were shopping at an antique store where they spotted a very ragged stuffed squirrel. Even with some fur missing, his eyes were bright and looked so life-like as he sat in an upright position with his paws stretched out; he was ready and willing to be adopted into our family as 'Earl The Squirrel'. I was chosen to be the first receiver, as 'The Brothers' made secret arrangements to introduce him to me at one of our Henkaline Christmas Parties. As the gift exchange began, The Baby Head found her new owner first ~ just before the GRAND surprise! The 'gag-givers' watched with great anticipation as I opened the beautifully wrapped box, where the little critter sat in all his splendor, staring up at me with his beady eyes, just waiting for me to scream! Those Brothers are very fortunate I didn't have a heart attack right there on the floor! Needless to say, Earl was the star of the gift exchange that year!

'Rocky, The Stuffed Raccoon' joined the family next. He was given to Laura (Chris' wife) from Ken and Julie. When she opened her prize, she let out a yell and almost threw the box across the room. Other choice surprises were added through the years; which included a ceramic pig with a pacifier in his mouth, a styrofoam lady bust, designed from the waist up, tagged as 'The Henkaline Door Knockers. And there was also The Black Mahogany Carved Woman's Head from Africa. Missie was the recipient of that beauty and proudly displayed her in her college dorm room. It became so popular that her roommate stole it for her own private collection and we never saw it again. That's alright! We didn't mind sharing.

The years have come and gone; enjoying all of our fun gift exchanges, but the 'Henkaline Head' will be the Grand-mama of them all! Now I encourage you to find a 'treasure' or two, to share and pass along to your special friends and family. I hope you enjoy this similar story, written by Patricia Lorenz, author of "The Yellow Shirt". As with us, it became a special bond for her loved ones. She gave us permission to tell how a yellow shirt became a special bond between a girl and her mother. The story also reminds me of the bond and love we share as a family throughout the year with our wonderful unusual Henkaline gifts. I encourage you to find a 'treasure' or two or three, to share and pass along with your loved ones.

39. THE YELLOW SHIRT – By Patricia Lorenze

The yellow shirt had long sleeves, four extra pockets trimmed in black thread and snaps up the front. It was faded from years of wear, but still in decent shape. I found it in 1963 when I was home from college on Christmas break, rummaging through bags of clothes Mom intended to give away. "You are not taking that old thing, are you?' Mom said when she saw me packing the yellow shirt. 'I wore that when I was pregnant with your brother in 1954!' It's just the thing to wear over my clothes during art class, Mom. Thanks! I slipped it into my suitcase before she could object. The yellow shirt became a part of my college wardrobe. I love it. After graduation, I wore the shirt the day I moved into my new apartment and on Saturday mornings when I cleaned. The next year, I married. When I became pregnant, I wore the yellow shirt during big-belly days. I missed Mom and the rest of my family, since we were in Colorado and they were in Illinois. But, that shirt helped. I smiled, remembering that Mother had worn it when she was pregnant, 25 years earlier. That Christmas, mindful of the warm feeling the shirt had given me; I patched one elbow, wrapped it in holiday paper and sent it to Mom. When Mom wrote to thank me for her 'real' gifts, she said the yellow shirt was lovely. She never mentioned it again. The next year, my husband, daughter and I stopped at Mom and Dad's to pick up some furniture. Days later when we uncrated the kitchen table, I noticed something yellow taped to its bottom. The shirt! And so the pattern was set. On our next visit home, I secretly placed the yellow shirt under Mom and Dad's mattress. I don't know how long it took for her to find it, but almost two years passed before I discovered it under the base of our living room floor lamp. The yellow shirt was just what I needed now while refinishing furniture. The walnut stains added character. In 1975 my husband and I divorced. With my three children, I prepared to move back to Illinois. As I packed, a deep depression overtook me. I wondered if I could make it on my own. I wondered if I would find a job. I paged through the Bible, looking for comfort. In Ephesians, I read, 'So use every piece of God's armor to resist the enemy whenever he attacks, and when it is all over, you will be standing up.' I tried to picture myself wearing God's armor, but all I saw was the stained yellow shirt. Slowly, it dawned on me. Wasn't my mother's love a piece of God's armor? My courage was renewed. Unpacking in our new home, I knew I had to get the shirt back to Mother. The next time I visited her, I tucked it in her bottom dresser drawer. Meanwhile, I found a good job at a radio station. A year later I discovered the yellow shirt hidden in a rag bag in my cleaning closet. Something new had been added. Embroidered in bright green across the breast pocket were the words 'I BELONG TO PAT.' Not to be outdone, I got out my own embroidery materials and added an apostrophe and several more letters. Now the shirt proudly proclaimed, 'I BELONG TO PAT'S MOTHER.' But I didn't stop there. I zigzagged all the frayed seams, and then had a friend mail the shirt in a fancy box to Mom from Arlington, VA. We enclosed an official looking letter from 'The Institute for the Destitute,' announcing that she was the recipient of an award for good deeds. I would have given anything to see Mom's face when she opened the box. But, of course, she never mentioned it. Two years later, in 1978, I remarried. The day of our wedding, Harold and I put our car in a friend's garage to avoid practical jokers. "After the wedding while my husband and I were in our honeymoon suite, I reached for a pillow to rest my head. It felt lumpy. I unzipped the case and found wrapped in wedding paper, the yellow shirt. Inside a pocket a note was written: 'Read John 14:27-29'. I love you both, Mother.' That night I paged through the Bible in a hotel room and found the verses: I am leaving you with a gift: peace of mind and heart. And the peace I give isn't fragile like the peace the world gives. So don't be troubled or afraid. Remember what I told you: I am going away, but I will come back to you again. If you really love me, you will be very happy for me, for now I can go to the Father, who is greater than I am. I have told you these things before they happen so that when they do, you will believe in me.' The shirt was Mother's final gift. She had known for three months that she had terminal Lou Gehrig's disease. Mother died the following year at 57. I was tempted to send the yellow shirt with her to her grave. But I'm glad I didn't, because it is a vivid reminder of the love-filled game she and I played for 16 years. Besides, my older daughter is in college now, majoring in art. And every art student needs a baggy yellow shirt with big pockets.

40. A Practical Joke Played On Wally

As I stated earlier, Wally was welcomed with warm affection to our family. As a part of the initiation process the brothers would bring Wally in on their good sense of humor. I remember this happened one time when we lived in Colorado Springs. Jack's and Jerry's Families came for a visit and Wally's full schedule at the base required him to work. Our kitchen sink had some dripping problems and Wally mentioned before leaving for work that he needed to call a plumber to stop the drip. After he left for work the brothers decided that it was a perfect opportunity to play a little practical joke on Wally. They shut the water off under the sink, found some wrenches to remove the water supply pipes and left the pipes and wrenches lying loose on the counter top. Then they took the garden hose from the back patio and ran it in through the kitchen window and coiled it in the sink. When Wally came home, I informed him at the door that the brothers were only trying to help but ran into a few problems trying to fix the kitchen sink drip. Jack was positioned in a chair with his hand wrapped with white gauze and ketchup stains. I told Wally, "He only had a small gash in his hand and we don't think it would take stitches."

Wally looked at the garden hose, the pipes and wrenches lying on the counter top and said in a very serious voice, "Why didn't you just let it alone and let me get it fixed with a plumber?" We all laughed and let him in our practical joke. Wally had a good sense of humor and allowed us to have fun at his expense. The brothers quickly reinstalled the pipes and allowed the leak to be repaired by a professional, and we all lived happily ever after.

41. Keeping The Record Straight

Being the eldest sibling in our family, I thought it might be my duty to critique some of The Brothers' written interpretations, because they love embellishing their tales! As a matter of fact, at each Christmas family celebration, our next generation listens to the same witty stories-of-the-past, roll their eyes, and then enjoy hearing the newest version that has been stretched beyond belief. We never have to guess whether it's fact or fiction. However, I must admit, as far as I know, their remarks listed in this book, have been amazingly on target.

42. The Purple Grape Pie

I was sure that our family was the first in the nation to have introduced the Famous Grape Pie. Mother always made our home smell so delicious on Bake Days. On one of those days, Popsy asked Mother to make a grape pie. She had never heard of such a thing, but to honor his request, she came up with a perfect recipe and from then on, it became one of our most favorite desserts.

My niece, Missie Henkaline Kogge had a tragic automobile accident on January 17, 2007. The day of Missie's accident we shared the sad news of her death with Bev, Keith and Ken. That night Bev dreamed that Missie and Mother were together in Heaven, baking grape pies for our relatives who had gone on before. I'm going to look forward to finding them in their Heavenly Bake Shoppe filled with all the grape pies we'd ever want to eat.

CHAPTER 3

Jerry Wayne Henkaline

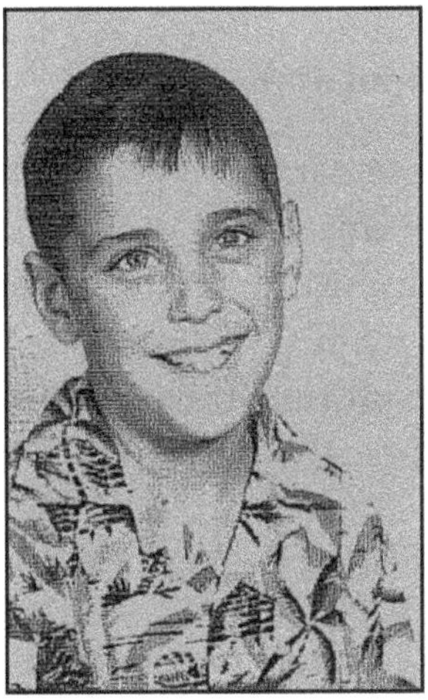

43. The Forts In The Woods

One of my favorite memories was when the brothers and I went to the woods and built forts in the trees. We used our wagon to carry all the necessary tools we needed for our projects. Once a month, Pops would have to make a trip back to the woods to collect all the tools we 'borrowed' to make our forts - hammers, nails, saws and squares that pulled our projects together.

44. Haymow Hiding Places

When the woods fort building was finished, we'd move to the barn to create tunnels and hiding places in the haymow. We'd make them so long that it was hard to breath and so dark that we couldn't see where we were going. So little Bro Kenny, who was the brains of our threesome, came up with the bright idea of using matches to light the way through the tunnels. The Man Upstairs surely was looking out for us, because miracle of miracles, the barn never burned down.

45. Black Diamond Liniment ....The Healing Medicine

Pop's had polio when he was a child. In his adult years, he would use Black Diamond Liniment to relieve the pain. This miracle liquid was also used to heal bruises and external pain. The smell was awful but the pain was relieved.

46. Thinning the Cat Population

We noticed we had an abundance of cats around the farm, so 'The Boys' thought we would thin some litters out. We had a nice big fireplace out in our yard, and we decided to start a fire and get some of the small, sickly ones and dedicate them for cremation. One of the stronger ones ran out of the fireplace and ran straight for the barn leaving a smoke screen behind! At that time, the 'party' was over! Again, the barn stood!

47. We Received Baby Chicks By Mail Order.

The mailman blew his horn and I ran out to see what he wanted. To my surprise there was a box with holes on the side and on top. I realized that it was making noises as I carried it into the house. I told Mother we received a box that was making noises. She laughed and said, "The chicks are here!" I thought they were little baby girls inside. Then to my surprise, Mother told me it was baby chickens that they ordered. I looked at Mother and said, "Let's get them out, I want to see what they look like." She opened the box and we found chirping little yellow chicks that were ready to become members of the Henkaline family. What they didn't know was their lives on our farm were on a limited time frame. Mother had plans for each one and the end was not going to be pretty.

48. The Hathaway House Wall Clock

I can't remember when the old Seth Thomas wall clock was not hanging on our dining room wall. It was just a part of the family and, like an old friend, did its job to tell us the correct time. Pops wound it every Friday night and we used it as our family US Naval Observatory Time Check.

Jerry Enjoying His Beauty Rest

49. One Scary Midnight Knock On The Door

It was a very bright moonlight night, as we were all in bed sleeping, when Mother and Pops heard three knocks on our basement entrance door. A few seconds later, the same three types of knocks were heard. It lasted for several minutes. Mother came into our bedroom and woke us up and said that Dad was going down with the shotgun to check this out. We were all very quiet and wide-eyed! A few minutes later Pops yelled upstairs and said it was our dog knocking his tail on the door that made the scary sound. After Mother cleaned all our pajama pants out, we all went back to bed and tried to get to sleep. (It was hard to get back to sleep because of the smell of all the dirty brown bottoms!)

50. Neighborhood Pastime Fun

Spending time at the Woodington School grounds was always fun. The school was located at the west end of Hathaway Road and at the intersection of State Route 49. We would arrive at the school on our bikes and then travel to other kids' houses to gather enough players to make two baseball teams. The school property was about three acres of grass with a two room school house. There was a baseball back stop in one corner and we provided our own bases. It was the batter's goal to hit the ball to the school house or over the property fence because they were close enough to complete the task with little effort. We would play until dusk and finally decide to go home. Our parents never worried about us out after dark and never thought about coming to look for us. We knew when to be home for a meal and the rest of the time was ours to find something to do. Many times, we made our own fun outdoors with our friends coming to Henkaline house on Hathaway Road. Those were great times and we had a great bond with our neighborhood friends.

51. Other Favorite Pastimes On The Farm

We were fortunate to have our own basketball rim that was attached to the barn that never burned down. I spent hours playing basketball games with the brothers, or just shooting for P-I-G or H-O-R-S-E. When friends and relatives visited we had a real basketball game with several players on each team. The rim was fastened to a wooden back board and the backboard was attached to a long wooden rail that pivoted from each side of the door opening. When we wanted to play basketball outside we swiveled the rim through the sliding door and the barn door made the back board. When it was raining or cold outside, we swiveled the back board to the inside and we played inside the barn. There was a light inside the barn so we could play our games after dark. It seemed 'The Henkaline Farm' was the center of attraction for lots of fun.

52. Pop's Rodeo Days

One Sunday after church, while our relatives were visiting and a couple of buddies from church were with us, Pops said, "Come out to the back lot and watch me ride the bull." He hopped on the bull's back and the bull just stood there. We figured it was his lucky day because the bull didn't make a move. Of course, we were told NEVER EVER to try such a thing! But one week later, 'The Boys' invited the neighborhood kids to watch our rodeo show out back riding the bull. Before the rodeo began, we didn't tell 'em we were going to ride a little steer. Once we came out of the barn on its back, with our feet touching the ground, the rodeo was over. Next week, we invited Pops out to watch our rodeo. After bringing the little bull out, with our feet on the ground, he realized his boys pulled a fast one on him.

53. Favorite Neighbors And Games We Played

The Snyder girls lived only a mile down the road from our house. *Mother May I* and *Hide and Seek* (in the barn), were two of my favorite games. One game I always tried to talk them into that they refused to play was when I wanted to be 'The Doctor' and give physicals because I was always so concerned for their health. They didn't buy it!

54. Favorite Saturday TV Shows

Rin-Tin-Tin, *The Rifleman*, *Lassie*, *Sky King and Howdy Doody* topped the list. On Saturday evenings, we watched Pop's favorite ... *The Lawrence Welk Show*. Through the week; *Father Knows Best*, *The Dick Van Dyke Show*, *I've Got A Secret*, *The Ed Sullivan Show* (where Elvis got his BIG break), *Leave It To Beaver*, and *The Mickey Mouse Show*, especially with our favorite Mouseketeer, Annette, added to the list.

55. Relatives At the House

Whenever aunts, uncles and cousins came back to the Darke County area they were always congregating at The Hathaway House. It was a fun, relaxed place to be. Mother prepared her customary great food. We would always get the ice cream maker out and make homemade ice cream. We would all take turns cranking the machine. We would always be playing basketball or baseball. With all the relatives there we had plenty of fun.

56. Friends At The House

Every weekend our home was the place where everyone congregated. Pops would walk out and the driveway would be full of cars. I think Pops enjoyed that as much as we did. There would be card games in the kitchen and of course Mother always had snacks for everyone to eat. They were both always willing to open their home to family and friends and really enjoyed taking part in all the fun. Anyone who didn't know where there kids were would either call or drive by. Chances were pretty good they were at the Henkaline's.

57. The Community Moped

One year I had a moped and the kids would meet at my house on their bicycles. We would leave the farm to go into town to play ball and they would all hook on with their bikes and I pulled them all into town.

58. The Fair

A special treat when we were younger was to go to The Great Darke County Fair one day each year. We were each given a dollar to spend and Mother would take a picnic lunch with cold chicken. Our family spent the whole day at the fair and always had our picnic lunch.

59. The Wonder Bread Truck Visits

Every other week, the Wonder Bread truck driver would come down Hathaway Road on his way to deliver bread to the Woodington Store. All three Henkaline boys would wait for the driver's arrival. He would drive up our driveway and wait for us to come out. We would purchase a Zero candy bar from one of the dimes of our allowance. Sometimes we would make a trade of vegetables from our garden and corn on the cob for our candy. This exchange method allowed us to save our precious money for other purchases. These special candy deliveries could only happen at the Hathaway house.

60. Dad's New Car Purchases

Pops always saved all his loose quarters and fifty-cent coins. He collected them in jars for purpose of his next car purchase. His car dealership was Elson Ford located in Versailles, Ohio. At the dealership he always went to his favorite salesman, Dick Berger. He trusted Dick and they became good friends. Dick would say, "When Bill Henkaline walked in the door I knew it was time to sharpen my pencil." He knew this was his job if he wanted to receive those jars of coins. When I became an adult, Dick and I became close friends and he shared how wonderful it was to recollect the "battle of their firm negotiations" for the final purchase price and the presence of the jars of many coins. Interestingly, Dick shared that Bill Henkaline was his favorite client. He said that he always loved those friendly encounters with such a wise businessman and knew that it would always turn into one of many successful sales. We can only imagine how many quarters and fifty-cent pieces, along with a trade, it would take to purchase a new $2,000.00 car. **Anita's Note:** I also profited from Popsy expertise when he helped me purchase a brand new 1960 Ford Falcon. Of course, the brothers were most certainly jealous because all they knew to do was to tell stories about how well I took care of my "Pride and Joy'.

Jack's Comments:

A few of the details describing the next three stories may have been slightly altered from the actual event as described by Jerry, due to lack of memory, or some unknown reason regarding the actual facts.

61. My Typing Class

We had a very small typing class at Ansonia Tech. At a very young age while learning to type on the manual typewriter, I had a vision the whole world should be in this classroom. I saw the world population using a method of typing using my invention of a product that would allow words to appear on a screen and project through thin air to others around the globe. I saw the potential of all walks of life using this method. As a result I taught others of my ideas and allowed the computer and World Wide Web to be invented. You will not see this as my idea in any public records. My feeling at this very young age was to not hold the world back with my creation and I do not expect any type of recognition. I am a little disappointed at this writing that Steve Jobs and Vice President Al Gore took full credit for my vision.

62. My School Days

Grades 1 through 6. My favorite subject was recess. I remember passing this class with solid "A's." After I reached high school, Gym became my favorite class. As I think back, Wilt Lynn was my favorite teacher in school because he was the Physical Education Teacher. We would spend numerous hours talking about all types of sports. At the end of my senior year, with all my research gathered, I determined I must have been instrumental in the invention of the Olympic Games. After further research, John F. Kennedy and I had a vision to create the Special Olympics. Some say I was a founding part of the Special Olympics. Although you will not find my name credited with either of these events, I personally feel this was the beginning of Olympic Games as you know them today.

63. Homework Memories

Through the week; after six hours of homework, we got to enjoy our favorite TV shows! And on Saturday afternoon, after two hours of Bible Study, we got to enjoy Saturday evening television. And of course on Sunday it was up for early morning breakfast and four hours of church and Bible Study before the boys could go out to play or watch any TV. Anita Comment: Jerry, your nose is growing.

64. My Shotgun Experience

The boys and Pop's took the 12 gage shotgun out for target practice. No one told me that I was supposed to hold the butt of the gun against my shoulder before I pulled the trigger. I held it about six-inches away, pulled the trigger and it nearly knocked me on my butt. That turned out to be the first and last time that I ever shot a shotgun.

65. Pop's Infantile Paralysis

A muscle and nervous system paralysis during his childhood caused Pops to have extremely arched feet. It was necessary for him to purchase special shoes in order to comfort the constant pain in his feet. They would severely swell at times but we never heard a word of complaint. Unless you noticed his shoes had high sides to support his balance you would never know there was a problem. Pops never wanted attention to his problem and went through his life working without any special favors or privileges.

66. My First Car

In 1960, the 1957 Chevy was the 'hot car' (and still is today as an antique model). I was talking with Pops about going car shopping and that I had my heart set on a 1957 Chevy. Pops found a 1956 Pontiac that was in great shape and shiny black. I don't know how he did it but he convinced me that this would be a nice first car for me. Of course he was right. It was one of the favorite cars of all my buddies and it served me well. After I broke it in, it was then passed on to Jack to enjoy. As always, Pop had the foresight to help us make the right decisions.

Pops Beside My 1956 Pontiac

67. School Sports

In basketball, I dressed varsity as a freshman and we went to the finals of the Darke County tournament. One particular game the coach said it looked as if we had all been ice skating all day. One of my friends on the team, Marvin Peters said, "I did." Then Terry Pepple said the same thing. We lost the game and the next day all we did was run during practice.

In baseball I played first base and did a little pitching. In track I threw the shot-put. Between Dave Muhlenkamp and me, we were always in the District Finals. No matter the sports season, after the games friends would head out to our house to rehash the game with Pops and eat more of Mother's cooking. Win or lose, they were always welcome.

68. Ansonia High School Football ...We Finally Won A Game

I played four sports while in high school and Mother and Pops would be at every game. I remember when Ansonia had the longest losing streak in the nation in high school football. We were seniors and were told that if we didn't win a game that year football would be dropped at our school. On Friday the 13th of September, 1963, we broke the losing streak. It was such big news that Uncle Wayne in Oregon heard it on a radio station and called Pops to see if it was the same Ansonia.

The Ooga-Booga play won the game and came right over me. I was playing tackle and at that time the tackles called the plays. I made the hole and Dave Muhlenkamp went right through for the score. After the game the parents got together and took the whole team to Dairy Queen for hamburgers and fries. Even though the DQ was closed, it was opened especially for us to celebrate the occasion. We went on to win three games that year, one against Minster.

It's Ended - Ansonia's Losing Streak Has Ended!

Senior Football Members

Tony

Jerry

John

Ed

Wayne

Tigers Blank Riverside, 6-0; Muhlenkamp Scores Touchdown

ANSONIA — "Tell the fans we don't believe in jinxes here," said Ansonia football coach Frank Bates after his big school football team defeated Riverside, 6-0, to end a 28-game losing streak dating back to 1958. The Tigers ended that ignonimous skein last night — Friday the 13th.

There were a determined bunch of Tigers — not black cats — who haunted the Riverside defense and scourged the invaders' defense to bring to a halt one of the longest losing streaks in modern-day football. Ansonia last won on Oct. 24, 1958, when the Tigers defeated Lakeview by the same score — 6-0.

Kenny

Doug

Terry

Jim

Mike

"There weren't any heroes," said Bates, "It was a fine team effort — a fine team effort all the way. Man, Ansonia's blowing apart."

It was Dave Muhlenkamp, a 6-1, 215-pound end who scored THE TD. He caught a two-yard pass from quarterback Tony Printz with four minutes remaining in the second period, and fell into the end zone for the game's only touchdown.

Drove 60 Yards

The play climaxed a 60-yard drive which began midway in the second quarter. The key play was a 25-yard keeper by Printz, who is in his third year as Ansonia QB.

Riverside threatened repeatedly throughout the contest, but couldn't push the pigskin into paydirt.

"Our defense did an outstanding job," remarked Bates, who was practically beside himself with happiness. "We worked really hard all week."

In the lineup for the Tigers last night were Muhlenkamp and Greg Whittington at the ends, Roger Schlechty and Jerry Henkaline at the tackles, Roger Young and Tim Barga at the guards. Dave Berger at center, Printz at QB, Wayne Harbison, and Dick Smith at the halfbacks and John Herron at fullback.

Streak Began In '58

Substitutions were Ralph Whittaker, Terry Wingler, John Wagner and Ed Riegle. These were the players who brought the word "Win" back to Ansonia football.

The streak began on Nov. 1, 1958 when the Tigers lost a 28-6 decision to Marion Local in the final game of that season. In 1959, '60, '61 and '62, the Tigers dropped nine games each year to extend the streak to 37.

Last week, Graham Local pounded the Tigers, 60-0, and the streak reached 38. But its' all over now.

"We'll be working hard again," Bates stated. The Tigers will have to be working hard since they'll be meeting Piqua Catholic in their Tri-County League season opener next Saturday night on the Miami Countians' gridiron. Game time is 8 p.m.

The linescore:

Ansonia	0	6	0	0	—6
Riverside	0	0	0	0	—0

SEPTEMBER 13, 1963

69. The Day I Wrecked My New Car

After high school, and with my first full time job, I purchased my first new car. It was a Pontiac Grand Prix that I owned for one whole day. It had been on order for four weeks and I was notified on a Friday I could pick it up from the dealer. It had a beautiful dark blue exterior with white interior with bucket seats. On Saturday evening, Terry Pebble, Marvin Peters, Jim Schumaker and I met up to cruise the town in Greenville. It was the first time Jim ever rode with me in any of my cars. It was raining that evening and after the second lap around, we were about 500 yards from Frisch's Restaurant. What we didn't see was a car out of control coming sideways towards us. The driver was drag racing and lost control of his car. He finally straightened the car out but could not keep it on his side of the highway. The car hit us head on and both car fronts went straight up in the air. The speed of the other car was estimated to be 75 mph. Jim was in the back seat and Marvin Peters was in the passenger front seat. Marvin bent down and hit his head on the dash. Jim flew over the front seat and through the windshield, and after impact was thrown back through the windshield into the car. Because the car was coming sideways before impact, nobody in my car knew what had happened. After the cars landed back on the ground, I tried to exit my car. The door barely opened. The interior lights came on and I looked into the back seat for Jim. What I saw was his face cut from the top of his ears to his chin. His teeth were exposed and he was bleeding terribly. The police were on the scene immediately and they pulled Jim from the car. There were many beer cans inside the other car and even more that had been thrown out.

Marvin, Terry and I had severe bruises but no severe cuts. The police asked the crowd that gathered for clean handkerchiefs to use as gauze. Jim was taken to the hospital first and we followed in other ambulances to be examined for injuries. Jim was immediately rushed into surgery. His mother and father were contacted and waited patiently for his condition. After a lengthy surgery, his mother was admitted in his room to see her son. She passed out from the sight of his face. Jim's stay in the hospital was lengthy and grueling. We knew later that the Good Lord was protecting all of us from death.

The Pontiac Grand After The Wreck

70. My Many Cars

While in my early 20's I had some favorite cars. The GTO with three deuces, the Chevrolet Corvette convertible and a new Pontiac Bonneville were my three favorite sets of wheels. The GTO created a problem. One Wednesday evening, the gang was sitting at our favorite gas station in downtown Ansonia, when we all decided to go our own way. I wanted to show the boys how the three deduces worked. On Main Street, I put the pedal to the metal and burned rubber halfway through town! As I was leaving Ansonia, heading south toward home on SR 118, I saw in my rearview mirror, the dreaded moving red lights from the Ansonia Police coming up behind me. I kept the pedal to the metal and those red lights kept getting smaller in my mirror, until I saw them no more. I proceeded home because it was bedtime. The next evening, I stopped again at our favorite gas station, met my friends, who told me the Ansonia Police had a warrant out for my arrest! After collecting my thoughts, I stopped in at the police station and asked what this warrant was about. 'Barney Fife' said that the night before, he had chased me out of town for speeding, but never caught me because of the high speed. I indicated to 'Barney' that I was in Greenville and never in Ansonia all evening. After discussing this matter with 'Barney', I told him he needs to catch the cars he's chasing, so I don't have to go through this again. I went back to the gas station and told the boys my story and we all got a big laugh out of that.

Jerry's Senior Picture

Jerry's 1965 Pontiac GTO

Jerry's Chevrolet Impala

Jerry And His Corvette

71. My Corvette

Playing softball, we had no way of smoothing the field for play. I became the solution by using my Corvette to pull a drag around the diamond. Who says that the Corvette is only good for looks and drag racing?

Jerry On A Fishing Trip

72. Work Years

After graduation I worked at Sheller-Globe in Union City and started R Lettering with Tom Everhardt. The R in R lettering stood for "OUR" because we could not agree on whose name should be first in the business. Transfers on shirts were a big thing and we decided we were going to cash in. We had a tee shirt in each size and a mix of colors when we made our first sale to Arcanum/Franklin Monroe little league. As far as they knew, we had a whole warehouse full of shirts. We could not afford the heat press machine to apply the transfers to the shirts so I stood on an iron to print them until we could afford to buy the machine. A year later I took over the business, rented a trailer, took vacation time from work and attended fairs to print tee shirts. While we still had R Lettering, I left Sheller-Globe just one day short of being there ten years. They were supposed to go on strike and I had a chance at another job in Minster so I went ahead and left. I quit my job on Friday and there was no strike on Monday. If I had clocked in that day I would have gotten my retirement.

We were selling most of the R Lettering merchandise in the Minster area and I decided to find a job in Minster. Dannon Yogurt was THE place to work at that time and I tried to get in there. Several months later, not hearing from Dannon, we were at Char's Grandpa Brucken's house in Ft. Loramie for the 4th of July and the owners of Dannon were next door at Clarence Meyer's (their brother). Al invited them over for a drink, introduced me and the following Monday I had the job. I started as a store door driver then went to sales after opening up the whole Indiana University area. Dannon wanted us to move to Indianapolis, but we did not want to leave Minster so someone else went. In a very short time they had hired 32 people to replace me and one other driver, Mike Goubeaux.

The first year we were married we lived in Versailles. Then we moved to Greenville. After Missie was born we moved to a house on Grey Avenue where we lived until Travis was born and I got the job at Dannon. At the time I got the Dannon job there were no homes for rent or for sale in Minster so we lived in Ft. Loramie next to Aunt Ebie for a year. R Lettering was in a renovated barber shop just two buildings away. Finally, a duplex on Main Street in Minster became available and we purchased our first house. We rented the upstairs apartment out to Bill and Brenda Young. We rented a building across from the post office for R Lettering. After a few years, when we were expecting Trent, we moved the business to the front room of our house. It was either grow the business and leave Dannon or sell it. Shortly after, we sold it to a Muhlenkamp family who eventually sold it to the Ernst family.

A few years later Ken and I started the first tanning bed studio in Auglaize County. That business was eventually sold to Ernst. There had been a lot of changes over the years at Dannon and while I was still working there Tom Meyer contacted me to work for him at Industrial Nameplates Division of Amos Press in Sidney as a salesman. After being there less than three years, Mark Nolan and Tom Barhorst who also worked there, and I decided to start our own company Trade Mark Designs. Each of the four kids, at some point, worked at the shop. Travis met his wife Jessica there, who was a temporary worker, and even, Wes and Taylor came to the shop and each earned their first paycheck from Grandpa. I owned the business for 16 years then sold my share to Ted Heckman. Prior to selling my share, I started another company, Recognition Awards, and later sold it to Ron Riethman. The building was sold to Ted.

73. Our Kids Growing Up

When the kids were growing up I was always coaching them in little league, Y basketball, or some sport. I also coached Minster High School Freshmen basketball one year as a community coach. I enjoyed seeing Missie and Travis in band together and watching each of them in school plays. Trent followed in my footsteps throwing shot in track and was a good football player. I will never forget the first time he kicked off. When he kicked his shoe went one direction and the ball in the other. Part of the St. Henry team went after the shoe. I cannot even count how many innings of baseball I watched Ty play through grade school, high school and Legion. All these activities kept us very busy, but I did have time to participate in two other notable events.

74. Mystic's Choice

While working at Dannon Yogurt another driver, his friend, and I bought a sulky racehorse named Mystic's Choice. My driver friend was responsible for all of the daily training and he and his friend were responsible for hauling the horse to the races each week, generally in Lebanon, Ohio. That pretty much left me responsible for paying the bills.

Of course at Dannon the two of us were teased constantly about the horse and everyone wanted to know when they were going to get to see it race. Finally, after we knew the horse was in good shape for an upcoming event, we made arrangements to take a couple vans of Dannon people down to the races. Needless to say the drive down was one hilarious comment after another from everyone who kept saying they were going to win enough off the race that night to retire.

When it came time for the race everybody from Dannon went and placed their bets, except me. But, when the race ended and Mystic had won, I was just as happy as the rest of them because good ole' Mystic performed her best at the best time and all our coworkers had to eat their words. Of course that was easy enough to do since they all made money on their winning tickets.

Mystic actually made us some money by placing him in certain races. Our scientific plan was to set him up in what is known as a 'claimer race' at Lebanon. It was our desire to have him in the lowest category in order for him to win. As a side note, the only way he couldn't win a race in this category was for him to drop over dead during the race.

The night of the claimer, as was tradition at the racetrack, each horse warmed up before their race. During the warm-up we noticed a horse limping. Sure enough, it was our horse! And of course it was announced that Mystic's Choice was scratched from the race. Our dreams were shattered! Now it was our duty to sell him or continue training him. We chose to put more money into our investment and continue training him with needed swim treatments.

The timing was a little off. Just the week before, when Char wanted to buy a family season pass at the swimming pool, I said, "No." When I came home and said I needed a check for Mystic to go to the swimming pool, which cost more for 45-minutes than the entire season pass for the family, in Char's mind, the horse was gone. At the same time, our other partner decided that we should buy his portion of the deal because he didn't want anything to do with the lame horse situation. There were a few strong conversations exchange in which he threatened to bring the horse over to our house and place him in the front yard. Missie thought it was a wonderful idea to have her own horse to ride around town with her friends and was jumping up and down on the bed chanting, "Mystic Is going to live here, Mystic is going to live here."

We finally all came to our senses and decided to sell our lame horse. Someone from Canada bought Mystic and after rehabilitation, he won his first two races. In the meantime, the kids enjoyed swimming all summer long. We have always wondered if our horse has become glue on an envelope by now.

75. The Mouse Game

One year, for the annual Minster Oktoberfest celebration two friends and I decided to build a "Mouse Game" to use to earn money for one of the parks in town. This was no small undertaking. We had a very large octagonal table built that spun and had Plexiglas sides. Around the entire outside perimeter were holes that would allow a live mouse to enter into a box below. Each of the sections was a different color and people could bet on the color paddles of their choice to try to win money. Under each of the sections was a drawer and we had a steel cover we could slide between the drawer and the table in order to keep the mouse trapped until we were ready to release it for the next spin.

One of the hardest things we had to do was gather live mice to use in the game. We finally put an ad in the paper and received phone calls so we picked up about 40 mice. We had stories about capturing each one. We set the table up for practice sessions at one friend's farm house. It was really good that we practiced. On the first spin, when we slid the lid over the drawer and pulled it out, we realized we needed an extra drawer to replace the one we were pulling. So that was the end of the first practice session. After having an extra drawer made, at the second practice session, we realized that not all mice wanted to play and some would just sit in the middle of the table while it spun instead of running to a hole. When they made no move, they were grabbed by the tail and flipped into the corn field. After eliminating several mice we realized we had to put peanut butter in each of the drawers to make them head to the holes and then all was well.

Finally, Oktoberfest arrived and we were the most popular stand. There were so many people watching they could not even get up to the stand to place their bets. One man from Dayton said he never had so much fun losing money in his life. We had so much money coming in we had to start putting it in coolers because it did not fit in our apron pockets. We did have a few casualties when a couple backup mice escaped and a real tragedy when we accidently beheaded one when we slid the lid in on top of the drawer. Needless to say, when it was time for the next spin and we dumped the drawer over for the mouse to start running, people were a little freaked out. We donated all of the profits to the new Paris Street Park in Minster which is really what got that park rolling. The town never even put a sign up about the donation made possible by the mouse game. A lot of mice left their homes and several gave their lives for that park

76. Pop's Prediction

Pop's said that our last child would be a boy. He passed away before Ty arrived. I know he would have been very proud of our new son and I wish he could have been here to see him.

77. Selling The Farm

I remember when the farm was sold Pops did not want to be there for the sale. That is when he seemed to lose part of his zest for life and his health started to waiver.

78. Closure Of Our Parents' Lives And Their Belongings

Pops died on August 25, 1983 and Mother died on April 18, 1984. We knew Pops death was gradually coming but Mother died with a sudden heart attack and left us in shock. After Mother's funeral we all gathered at her apartment to finalize the Folk's earthly belongings and close the ties of the important chapter of our lives. We began by contributing portions of their clothes to church and charity establishments. While living, our parents told each of us that it was very important to them that there would be no fighting between siblings over any possession they left behind. We talked about this at the gathering and agreed to meet their wishes. There would be no hard feelings and no fighting over anything.

We finally decided the best process would be to conduct a personal auction. The first step was for all to agree on a fair price for each item. We logged all the items and then agreed upon a fair price. Next we wrote our name on identical small papers and folded them. As the process began we had to decide if we wanted to have the opportunity to purchase the item at the price we previously established. As the item was brought forward, each of us voiced our special requests for that item and if we wanted the item, our name would be placed in the bowl for the draw. If our name was drawn from the bowl, we were awarded the item for the price we earlier established. Finally we decided to take turns pulling the papers from the bowl. As we looked around we determined we were dealing in some pretty 'high finance' and that we needed some type of tool to guide us. Char suggested we needed to get out the Monopoly Game and use the play money for visual guidance to illustrate how much each person was spending on the items.

Before the auction began, we marveled that the one and only item that each of us really wanted was the Family Grandmother Clock that was hanging on the living room wall. It was agreed that the clock would be the last item to be finalized. Of course at this point, we all knew that when everything was said and done it was completely unnecessary to complete this transaction because Jack always ended up getting most of the treasures. What can we say, other than some people have all the luck! It was time for the auction to proceed. When all items had been auctioned, of course Jack's name came up on most to cast his bid, it was time to draw the name for the clock. We were tired and decided to take a little break before the last name was to be drawn from the bowl for the clock. When we returned to the living room for the final draw, Ken was standing in front of the clock in amazement. He brought us all together and stated "The clock stopped just minutes before." Cold shivers were running down our spines at what we were seeing. Jerry finally said that Mother and Pops were sending a message to us all that they are proud of us for handling everything with the love and honesty that they had instilled in all our lives. And by the way, Jack's name was drawn for the clock. No one was surprised.

The Seth Thomas Wall Clock

An interesting sideline in this event was that our cousin Jim Shiverdecker came by the house to make sure we were doing okay and when he entered he saw all the play money laying on the floor. Jim stated, "What are you doing?" We did the best we could to explain, but we think he could not comprehend the process we were using to complete our parent's final wishes.

CHAPTER 4

Jack Blaine Henkaline

79. Daddy's Dream Came True

Before I was born, Mother and Daddy lived in a rental house on Windrick Pike which is east of Union City, Indiana. They paid a portion of their rent by cleaning their landlords' house and washing their dinner dishes. Mother told us their landlord and his wife would leave the dinner table with food still on their spoons and forks. Mother would clean the food from the silverware and wash them before placing them in the storage drawer. They did this labor so they could save enough money to buy a small farm to raise their family. Daddy worked in Greenville at the

Hobart Kitchen-Aid Mixer factory and mother was the homemaker. When they saved enough money for a down payment, Daddy found the farm on Hathaway Road. He made an offer on the property and went to the bank to apply for a loan. The 56 acre farm consisted of a house, a large barn, a detached garage, a tractor barn, several small chicken houses and other out buildings. My dad's brother-in-law, Charlie Shiverdecker learned of the upcoming deal and immediately came to see him. Daddy was told that times were hard and advised him not to go into debt. We were told that Charley stated, "Where will you live if you lose the farm?" My daddy quickly said, "We are not going to lose the farm." The entire farm was finally purchased for less than $5,000.00. and this was the beginning of our stories on Hathaway Road.

the purposes therein mentioned.

IN TESTIMONY WHEREOF, I have hereunto subscribed my name and affixed my official seal, on the day and year last aforesaid.

(N.P. name on)
(Notorial Seal)

Charles F. Bazata, Jr.
Notary Public of New Jersey
My commission expires July 31st, 1945

$5.65 Rev. stamps attach. & canc.
Trans. Jan. 5,1944
Filed Jan. 5, 1944, at 1:55 P.M.
Recorded Jan. 6, 1944.
Fee 35¢

Carl Miles ______ Recorder
Maxine Miles ______ Deputy

-----0-----

No. 19469 - George W. Miller et ux to William H. Henkaline et ux

WARRANTY DEED

KNOW ALL MEN BY THESE PRESENTS: That George W. Miller (married man) of the Village of Ansonia, County of Darke and State of Ohio in consideration of the sum of One Dollar and other valuable considerations to them paid by William H. Henkaline and Olive Henkaline of the Township of Brown, County of Darke and State of Ohio the receipt whereof is hereby acknowledged, does hereby GRANT, BARGAIN, SELL AND CONVEY to the said William H. Henkaline and Olive Henkaline their heirs and assigns forever, the following REAL ESTATE, situated in the County of Darke in the State of Ohio and in the Township of Brown and bounded and described as follows:

Being the west half of the south half of the north west quarter of section Thirty-three (33), Township Thirteen (13), Range Two (2) East, Containing Forty (40) acres of land be the same more or less.

TO HAVE AND TO HOLD said premises, with all the privileges and appurtenances thereunto belonging, to the said William H. Henkaline and Olive Henkaline their heirs and assigns forever.

And the said George W. Miller for himself and his heirs, do hereby covenant with the said William H. Henkaline and Olive Henkaline their heirs and assigns, that he is lawfully seized of the premises aforesaid; that the said premises are FREE AND CLEAR FROMALL INCUMBRANCES WHATSOEVER; and that he will forever WARRANT AND DEFEND the same with the appurtenances unto the said William H. Henkaline and Olive Henkaline their heirs and assigns, against the lawful claims of allpersons whomsoever.

IN WITNESS WHEREOF, the said George W. Miller and Gertrude M. Miller, his wife who hereby release her right of dower in the premises, have hereunto set their hand's, this 4th day of January, 1944.

Signed and acknowledged in presence of

Pearl Summers — George W. Miller
J. L. Harrison — Gertrude M.Miller

THE STATE OF OHIO, DARKE COUNTY, SS.

BE IT REMEMBERED, That on this 4th day of January, 1944, before me, the subscriber, a Notary Public in and for said county, personally came the above named George W. Miller and Gertrude M. Miller (Husband and Wife) the Grantor's in the foregoing Deed, and acknowledged the signing of the same to be their voluntary act and deed, for the uses and purposes therein mentioned.

IN TESTIMONY WHEREOF, I have hereunto subscribed my name and affixed my official seal, on the day and year last aforesaid.

(Notorial Seal)

John L. Harrison
Notary Public
John L. Harrison, Notary Public
Commission expires 6-27-1944.

$8.80 Rev. stamps attach.& canc.
Trans. Jan.5, 1944.
Filed Jan. 5, 1944, at 1:51 P.M.
Recorded Jan. 6, 1944.
Fee 90¢

Carl Miles ______ Recorder
Maxine Miles ______ Deputy

-----0-----

Property Deed – Miller To Henkaline On Hathaway Road

80. Basement Steps Adventure

I had my share, and I think everybody else's share, of accidents in our family. I recall a time when the boys were playing on the basement stairway landing one Sunday night. Somehow I fell down the steps. My daddy was sitting in the living room not knowing what we were doing at the time of the fall. When Jerry saw me lying unconscious at the bottom of the stairs, he casually walked up to Dad in the living room and calmly said, "Jackie fell down the steps." My daddy came running and found me unconscious on the basement floor with a cut on my head. He did not think the cut was too serious so a doctor was not needed. I still have a scar on my forehead to remember this one.

81. Anita And The Swing

Another time my sister Anita was swinging me on a swing located in the front yard. The swing was very unusual because the metal pole frame was about 20 feet high. This design allowed the rider to really swing out and reach high altitudes. I think Anita's goal was to test the swing out to maximum height with me on it. She positioned herself behind the swing and began pushing me out. When the swing got to her height, she began jumping to swing me higher. Soon I felt like I was in the tree tops. It was then that I lost my balance and fell off backwards in the bushes. Luckily, I only had the wind knocked out of me and was up and running in just a few minutes.

82. Daddy's' Stick

Dad used a tobacco lathe as a kid correction tool. It was about 2' long, 1" wide x ¼" thick. It had a brown smooth surface like a fine antique. I can't remember when it wasn't there so I assume that God made it from a tree in the Garden of Eden and gave it to Dad later. You can read about the tree and where the stick might have come from, in Genesis 1: 12. Anyway, back to "The Stick". The famous stick was kept in the basement entry landing just off the kitchen. When its presence was made, the boys knew the rule. There were no more warnings. Dad did not say, "I'm going to count to three and you had better behave. He just got up, walked to the basement entry to retrieve the stick and returned to his place with it in his hand. When he was really upset with us he would slam it down beside him. That really scared the crap out of us boys. There were times when we tested this little rule and the stick was used on our back side with a couple of whacks. Even stupid kids could learn from this experience the next time. Most of the time its presence was all that was needed.

83. Our Dusty Gravel Road

Hathaway Road was a gravel road for most of the years of my childhood. During the dry summer days the dust would fly high in the air as the cars drove by and it slowly settled to the surrounding trees, bushes and the ground. Our front door was always closed to keep the road dust from entering our living room. I remember many times when a big black oil tanker would come by and spray the entire road with used motor oil to cause the dust to cling to the road. Sometimes Daddy would call the road maintenance crew if the oil wore off and the dust became too much of a nuisance. Within a few days that old oil tanker would show up again on our road to lay down more of that used motor oil. I wonder what EPA would think of this technique today. I can imagine an EPA call being made and men showing up in white suits and oxygen masks with tanks attached to their backs to test the soil. I am sure they would demand a 30 inch deep section of the road surface be removed and taken to a contamination site for hazardous waste. Isn't it strange that I don't recall having any health problems from anybody living on our road in those days? My, how times have changed.

84. The Hair Cut

At one time, we went to Greenville to visit a Barber Shop to get our hair cuts. The original hair style began as a Porcupine Butch which looked like short hair overall except for a short clump of hair at the forehead area. The hair stood up straight with the help of a product called "Butch Wax". It was a grease product and did the trick to tame the little patch of hair in the front. When we became teen agers we graduated to the "Flat Top." This was a short cut except for a line of hair standing up around the side and front of the head. Again, "Butch Wax" was used to keep the hair up and straight.

Eventually Daddy decided to save some money and bought a pair of hair cutting clippers with accessories. This home cut event took place in our kitchen where we were required to sit on a red high chair on a week night. Daddy was a perfectionist and he took his good old time on each head to get it right. If he slipped up and caused a nick in the hair, he spent as much time as he needed to blend it in. The time on the high chair seemed like an eternity for me, but his hair cut was always good.

Jerry - Jack – Kenny With Those Snazzy Pineapple Butch Hair Cuts

85. The Shared Bedroom

A room that gives me some very special memories was my bedroom. It was a large room that was shared with my two brothers. It was located on the second floor and the second largest room of the house. The size of this room was enough for three beds and still plenty of empty space to move around. The room was heated by the use of an open floor register which allowed the gravity of heat to enter from the downstairs living room. Because there was no forced heat entering the room the temperature became pretty cold during the winter months. Many nights you could see your breath in the air. To keep warm, our beds were layered with many blankets. They kept us toasty warm during the coldest of winter nights. My brothers and I wore flannel pajamas and sometimes even a hooded sweat shirt to help stay warm. We would enter the upstairs through a hallway door and run to our beds to get under the mountain of blankets. Only the top of our heads could be seen but soon the bed became all warm and cozy from our body heat. We would then fall off to sleep knowing that we were safely tucked in our beds and protected from the outside cold. I think the cold room helped us fall asleep. Some nights there were sounds that entered our bedroom caused by cold wind passing by our television antenna located beside the windows on the south side of the room. This wind made strange humming sounds as the heavy winds came around. The sound would change from a low pitch to a high frequency. These strange sounds were not too loud and actually fun to listen to as we waited for our sleep to arrive. In the warmer season, at night, the windows were opened to allow the cool breeze to enter and pass through the upstairs rooms. The open windows also allowed us to hear the trains pass by in nearby Woodington, Ohio. I had perfect visions of the trains as I heard them passing through the country side. The railroad tracks were located about two miles away and the train sounds were pleasant to hear. We anticipated the whistle blow before the train crossed the highway beside the Woodington elevator. I could hear the clickety-clack of the railroad cars on the tracks and the distant rumble of the engine. I would envision the train in my mind as the sounds entered our room. This usually would put me to sleep. Our bedroom was a great place to go at the end of the day because it was a peaceful, safe and a restful place which allowed my mind to explore unlimited thoughts and places before I fell off to sleep.

86. Arms Through The Pockets

I had a habit as a child to wear my trousers high and above the waist. My fat little belly gave the waist of the pants a nice resting place and the belt above my belly was very comfortable and a great way to keep my pants from sliding down. My brothers would often state, "Why don't you just cut holes above the side pockets of your pants and run your arms out the holes". I didn't care what they said; if it felt good you had to do what you had to do to stay comfortable. Another benefit of this was that I looked unique from the other kids.

Jack
Check Out Those High Pants

87. The All Purpose Cold Medicine

If we had a cold, a sore throat, a running nose or chest congestion, Mother would bring out the dark blue glass bottle of Vick's Vapor Rub. She would stick her finger in the bottle and pull out a glob of the all purpose congestive ointment to apply to our body. In other applications, the nose was plugged with it, the chest was rubbed with it and the mouth swallowed a hunk of it. If none of this worked she would put a glob of Vicks on a flannel cloth and pin it to our jammies over our chest. Vicks was the "All-In-One" miracle drug for any cold.

88. The Coal Furnace

We heated the house with coal. In the basement you would find a big furnace that had a heavy cast iron entry door on hinges. We would lift the cast iron door handle and pull it open to see the internal fire and coal burning. The coal was automatically fed in the furnace by an auger under a machine called a stoker. The stoker would hold the coal and the auger would take the coal to the furnace when the thermostat in the living room called for more heat. If you had the furnace door open when the thermostat called for more heat, the blower would kick on and you could see the fire rising up. The heat would force you away from the opening until you closed the chamber door. We had the coal delivered a couple times each winter season by dump truck. The coal entered the house by way of an outside basement window. The dump truck would back up to the side of the house and the driver would place a metal chute from the truck tail gate into the window opening. The coal would enter into a large area of the basement floor which was bordered by a short wooden fence. The fence would contain the coal from the rest of the basement. The height of the coal in this area was about 3 feet high. Our job was to fill the stoker each night with coal. We would shovel the coal into a bucket and pour it into the stoker. The stoker supply would last about two days. The final job was to remove the unburned remains of the coal from the internal furnace floor. You did this by opening the door and using a long handled set of "C" clamps to grab each mineral deposit called a clinker. It was a hard "rock like" cluster that had to be removed to allow new coal to enter the furnace floor and burn to make more heat. We placed the clinkers in a bucket to cool, and then later took them out to the driveway. They would become broken into small pieces as our car would run over them and help replace the driveway gravel. I can still remember being outside at dusk during the cold winter months and watch the black coal smoke slowly rise from the chimney. I would smell the aroma of the coal being burned and knew that my home was warm and toasty inside. You can call it EPA Dirty Emissions, but I call it good old cozy heat aroma.

Daddy Relaxed On The Hathaway Side Porch

89. The Back Patio

Just before entering the enclosed back porch, you could find a cement floor patio that was used to enjoy the view of the front yard and the barnyard. On a Sunday afternoon, you could find my parents enjoying the weather from this location. When company came on a Sunday afternoon, this is where our family and guests would gather to enjoy their conversation and relax. In the picture above, you can see my Daddy enjoying a sunny day. There were flowers and pretty trees placed around the patio. Also in the background was our chicken house.

90. The Carbon Film

We had several boxes of carbon film stored in the upper kitchen cabinets. I don't ever remember anybody using the carbon film for any practical work. For fun we would take two sheets of paper and sandwich the carbon film in between. I found it amazing that the letters and numbers would transfer from the top sheet to the sheet below. I guess this was the early version of the Xerox Copy Machine.

91. Greeting Daddy Home From Work

Daddy worked as an inspector at Hobart's Manufacturing in Greenville, Ohio. This was where Kitchen Aid mixers were manufactured. Since Greenville was about ten miles from our home, Dad shared a car pool with my cousins Thurman and Jim Shiverdecker. Daddy came home around 4:00 pm every day. At least one of the boys would usually go out to greet his car coming up the driveway. When I was about nine years old, I decided to wait at the end of the driveway on my bike for Daddy's arrival. My plan was to ride beside his car as an escort as he drove up the drive. As I saw his car approaching, I took my position near the road. As he rounded the corner into our driveway, my bike and I followed the pattern of his car on the grass. As his car was heading up the driveway, I was standing up as I rode so I could look through the passenger window and see my Daddy. When Daddy saw this he was amused. As he reached the top of the driveway and got out of the car, he began to wonder where I was. It didn't take him long to find me laying unconscious beside a tree next to the driveway. I forgot where the tree was located and I ran into it head-on as I peered through the car window. Some kids just aren't too smart at times.

92. The Friday Night Treats

Daddy's Friday night arrival was always a special event. The boys knew that he got paid on Friday's and on his lunch hour he would walk to downtown Greenville to the bank to deposit his check into his checking account, put some money in the Christmas club account and end up at the GC Murphy store to buy several varieties of candy. He would buy at least three different generous sacks and the boys would be watching the clock like vultures for the candy raid.

93. The Candy Raid That Went Bad

There was one Friday we were all keyed for the candy arrival. Each of the boys secretly planned to get to the sacks first for the choice candy. We were sitting in the living room watching television when my brother

Jerry, sensed Daddy's arrival. He rocketed off like a light to meet daddy and I was close behind. When we got to the back porch door, Jerry decided to slow me down by swinging the door shut just as I arrived. I tried to push the door back open using a straight forearm. My hand missed the door and pushed straight through the glass. Mother heard my scream and came running to my rescue. What she found was a large gash on my right forearm where the skin was laid open with blood streaming out. She quickly ran for white towels and wrapped them tightly around my bleeding forearm. What Jerry learned was that it was not Daddy coming but a car passing our house. Since we had only one car and my Dad was driving it, we had to wait until he came home to take me to the hospital for stitches. He arrived home that night about one half hour late because he had to work overtime. When my daddy finally came home, I was rushed to the doctor's office to get the needed stitches. I still have the scars as a remembrance of the event. I don't recall Jerry offering me the best candy when I returned home from the doctor.

94. The Dinner Table

Eating at the dinner table was some experience. The Kitchen Aid mixing bowl full of fresh mashed potatoes was a standard along with a meat and vegetable dish. Mother was a great cook and even now, as I recall these memories, I really miss her home cooked meals. The meal always began with Daddy saying the prayer while the boys peeked across the table to see what food they could grab first. We always ate like starving pigs and never left the table hungry. Sometimes Daddy would push meat off his plate onto ours if one of us complained that somebody got more than the other. Occasionally there would be an argument at the table between the boys. Daddy would only allow the bickering to go on for a short time before he would walk to the basement stairway and get the tobacco lathe. It only took one slam of the stick on the table for him to restore order. It was amazing to us at the time how that little stick had so much influence on our behavior.

95. Jerry Going To School

In his younger years, Jerry made it perfectly clear that he did not like to go to school. Kenny and I quickly learned this when he would cry his eyes out, and yell out, "I don't want to go to school!" Mother would try and reason with him before the bus arrived but usually had to shove him up the bus steps while the bus driver quickly closed the door behind him. Anita would shutter in embarrassment and pull him back to his seat. Kenny and I would watch from the front window in amazement. I think Jerry got more comfortable around his senior year of school about boarding the school bus.

96. The Broken Window

I don't remember my age, but my guess is that I was about 7. I was playing with a little toy work bench that we received as a Christmas present. It was a simple toy which consisted of a 12 inch long surface with legs about 6 inches high. The flat surface was centered on the legs and had 6 small holes. The object was to take a wooden hammer and drive 6 wooden pegs into the holes. To remove the pegs, all you had to do was turn the work surface upside down and hammer the pegs in the opposite direction until they fell out. This game got boring after a few cycles and would be tossed aside to play with something else. I remember that I was playing with the workbench one morning in the kitchen when Kenny decided it was his turn. He grabbed the workbench away from me and took off running. I still had the hammer in my hand and immediately used it as a flying projectile toward Kenny as he was running away with my toy. The hammer missed my target, his head, and went flying towards the kitchen window. It hit the glass and took a small section out of the window. Mother heard the crash and came into the room to see the broken window. She turned to me and said, "Why did you break the window?" Knowing not to say the hammer missed my target, I immediately said, "It's cold outside, I wanted to let the birdies in." I don't think she bought the story but looking back on the event, I think I did pretty well when it comes to "Thinking Fast On Your Feet."

97. Another Fall For Jack

Another time I remember falling was a church party in the Greenville, Ohio City Park. The kids were climbing a very tall slide as fast as they could and running back for the next climb. I climbed the steps to reach the top and quickly slung my bottom on the slide surface and fell off.

As I look back on all these experiences, I have come to believe that I was very clumsy as a boy and am very lucky to be alive today.

98. Our Weekly Allowance

As we got older from childhood we were given responsibilities. Feeding the livestock, filling the furnace stoker with coal and mowing the yard were examples of some of the chores we were given. One day Daddy announced that he was going to give us an allowance for our work around the house. I wasn't old enough to go anywhere and everything was provided so I didn't even think about having any money of my own. I remember Daddy saying, "I am going to give you boy's a weekly allowance for doing the chores. How much do you think you should receive? I thought for a minute and said, "How about a penny per day). Daddy said, "How about 25 cents a week?" I said, "Are you sure that isn't too much?" He told us that the amount was fine and I thought I was rich. I dreamed the whole next week of what I could do with all that money. Haven't times changed?

99. The Drag Race When Kenny Was The Star Player

Anita was frequently asked to sing vocal solos at church and weddings. There was one time when Mother agreed to drive Anita to a practice of one of these events. It was a summer evening and I think Mother would use any excuse to get away from her hellion boys. That evening there was not much going on so the boys decided to hang outside and pester Anita and Mother before they left for the practice event. As they were pulling out of the driveway in the car, Kenny went brain dead and decided to run behind the car as he was grabbing the rear bumper. Mother started out by driving slowly so this was an easy trick for Kenny. Jerry saw what was going on and decided to run along side the car and look in the window. When Anita saw him, she turned to Mother and said, "Speed up and let's get away from him." Mother did just that and Jerry and Kenny ran faster to keep up. Anita said, "Faster, faster, go faster." They passed ahead of Jerry as he saw Kenny being drug behind the car. Kenny was hanging on to the bumper and he was afraid to let go. Jerry began to scream as loud as he could for them to stop. Sensing something was terribly wrong, they stopped the car and Kenny dropped

off. They found him laying face down with the tops of his ankles raw from being drug along the gravel road. Observing what had happened, I think Anita might have said, "Leave him there, I'm going to be late," but Mother would have nothing to do with that. Mother took him back to the house for medical treatment and he had to dress the wounds and wear white bandages and white socks for several weeks.
(**Anita's Note:** Just another example of wild extravagant story telling by one of my brothers.)

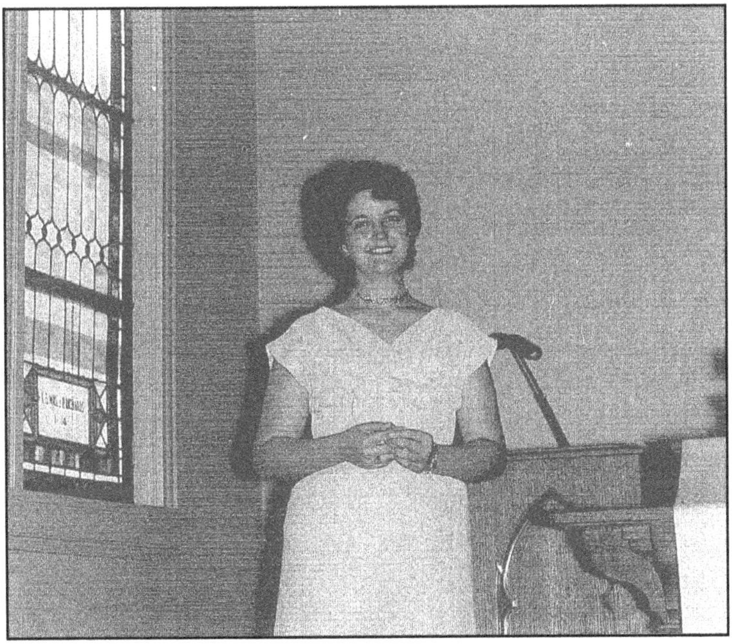

Anita Preparing For Solo At Church

100. Running Around The Table

My two brothers and I would push Mother's sanity to the maximum. Fights between the boys would break out and cause her anger to exceed the limits. After her failed attempts to get things back under control by yelling at us, she would go to the basement step landing and get the tobacco lathe to gain control. We did not fear her like we did my Daddy, so many times we would continue to misbehave even with the stick in hand. Mother came after us with the stick flying around in her hand. We would head for the dining room table to begin the race around the table away from her. Since we were much faster than her, we could complete the table lap and end up chasing her. Once she sensed we were close behind her, she would turn around and chase us in the opposite direction. She finally would wear out and give up the chase. It was then she would tell us that Daddy would deal with us when he came home. This got our attention and caused us to straighten up for the remainder of the day, hoping she would forget about her threat. She usually did.

101. Laundry Day

Mother would round up all the dirty clothes every week and take them to the basement to be put in her manual Maytag washing machine. This Maytag had an open tub with an agitator in the middle. There was no automatic stop or cycle options. She put the clothes in the tub, turned it on and washed them for a specific time. Afterwards she drained the tank of soapy water and used a hose to fill her tub with rinse water. Once she complete the agitated rinse cycle, she took each article of clothes and ran them through a hand motorized wringer to remove the excess water. Her dryer was the clothes line in the yard. There were several clothes lines and she would attach each article with two clothes pins to the line and let Mr. Sun do the drying. Later in the day, it was time to take the cloths off the line and put them in a clothes basket. Mother would bring her dried clothes into the house for folding and ironing. There was no permanent press material in those days so she would get out her iron and ironing board to press out the wrinkles for the clothes we wore. I can still smell the fresh bed sheets that Mother placed on my bed each week after she washed and dried them on the clothes line. The sheets had a crisp feel and a wonderful aroma that I loved. At the time, I did not appreciate all the hard work my mother did for us to keep us clean and healthy.

102. Rainy Day Fun

When rainy days came around, my Mother would allow us to get out the bed sheets and spread them over the living room and dining room furniture to make tents. We would crawl around in the covered areas and play with our toys. It wasn't long before we became bored and left the sheets hanging for Mother to put away. I think she would do anything to keep us occupied for a few minutes and away from her to complete her busy chores.

103. A New Pet Playmate

There was always something to get into on the farm. Although we owned a small farm in perspective, it really seemed like a lot of land to me in my early childhood. When the boys ran out of normal things to do we looked for the unusual. One summer morning, when school was out, we were delighted to find a new pet near the house. It was a possum that didn't seem to be afraid to come running up to us. We thought this was pretty neat but because of its ugly looks, we wouldn't let it get too close. It would run after us and we would run just fast enough to not allow it to catch up. After awhile we got tired of running just ahead of the pet, so we went to the barn and hooked up a little flat bed wagon to the garden tractor. We then let our new found friend chase us under motor power for awhile. This was fun because he would run after it but wasn't quite fast enough to catch us. Soon this also became old and one of us went into the house to get mother to watch us play with our little pet. Mother immediately realized that wild animals would never approach a human let alone chase one. Since Daddy was at work, she quickly told us to go across the road and get our neighbor, Emmitt Welch. He observed what was happening and got his gun to shoot the possum in the head. Later we learned that the possum probably had rabies and if it would have bitten us, we would have been infected with the virus. This was just another day the Good Lord was watching over the Henkaline boy's.

104. Our Dog Tippy

We always had many cats and a dog on the farm. Tippy was a black border collie with a white shield just below his neck. He was a fun dog to have around. I remember one time when he followed us back to the woods. While we were there, a bull came into the woods from an adjoining field. The bull ran after us and we quickly climbed a big tree. Tippy was right there with us and stood at the bottom of the tree barking at the bull. The bull got very mad and would not go away. We kept cheering for Tippy from the tree limbs. We weren't smart enough to know the bull was not mad at us, he was mad at Tippy. Finally Tippy and the bull got tired of each other and the bull went away. At the time, Tippy was our hero and we thought he saved our lives. Our time with Tippy finally came to an end when he chased one too many cars on our road and was hit and killed in front of our house.

105. The Pup Who Did Not Make It

Another dog story relates to a litter of pups. I was very young at the time and I don't remember which dog was the mother, but we were blessed with many puppies. We often would play in the barn and I wanted to pull one of the puppies in the haymow to play. I remember taking a rope and tying it tight around the puppies neck. I climbed the make shift ladder with the loose rope in my hand. When I reached the haymow floor I pulled him up to me. I really couldn't understand why he was dead when he reached me.

106. Our Dog Lassie

Lassie was another dog that we owned. He was an adult border collie and the best and smartest dog we ever had. We found Lassie at a farmer's house where we were employed to help bring in the hay from the field. The farmer showed us his dog and told us that he was looking for a good home for the dog. When we returned to our home, we told our parents about the dog and how smart he was. The next day Daddy took us back to the farmer's house to look at Lassie. He was impressed with the dog and we took Lassie home. Kenny taught Lassie all kinds of neat tricks and she gave us much love and companionship. I remember that Lassie still lived on the farm after I got married and moved away.

107. The Garden

When you look at the Cover Page you will see a large plot of ground on the south side of the house that we used as a garden. It was huge enough that Daddy would use the tractor and disk to work the ground. We grew tomatoes, green beans, lima beans, peas, beets, sweet corn, popcorn, lettuce, cabbage and other vegetables. In the summer mornings the boys were told to get out of bed and pick the vegetables or hoe the weeds. I remember one particular morning when we were sound asleep and mother wanted us in the garden. She came into the bedroom and yelled, "Get out of bed, it's too hot to sleep." At the time it didn't make much sense but we got up. At night, mother would sit in her swivel chair and snap beans while watching television. She would also ask us to help and we would sit with her as we opened the pea pods and peeled the pea out for freezing. After the harvest, she would get her pressure cooker out from storage and can all types of garden vegetables for the coming winter months. These were good times in our family.

108. The Clubhouse

One of the greatest ideas that we ever came up with during our childhood days was the clubhouse. It was a small building close to the tractor barn which originally was used as a chicken house. It sat empty for several years and Kenny and I saw an opportunity for our private place to sleep out. We got permission to use it and cleaned it out by scrubbing it down with Lysol soap and water and finally using a powerful disinfectant cleaner my mother provided. After the cleaning was inspected and approved for usage, we were in business. We needed electricity so we strung a heavy electrical cord from the tractor shed to our new club house. We installed electric lights, and eventually we used the electrical power to install an old electric motor with a blade to create a ventilation fan.

We had some very memorable times in that club house. Our cousin Terry Shiverdecker would come over on a Friday night and we would bake a store boxed pizza and watch "*Outer Limits*" and the "*Twight Zone*" on television. By this time it was ten o'clock and time to head out to the clubhouse. Before coming over, Terry would sneak dirty magazines from his dad's private collection and we would look at them and have some very interesting conversations as we viewed the naked girls. I don't remember my parents telling us about the birds and the bees, so I guess this was our first experience for self introduction to our sex education classes. All this conversation made us hungry again so we would head back to the house for some popcorn and Kool Aid. After stuffing our mouths we would head back out to our club house to see more of those interesting magazines. Some nights, if the moon was bright, we would roam our fields and the surrounding neighborhood. There were times when we went back to our woods to see what it looked like at night. If the moon was shining bright through the tree's it made the woods a very scary place to be. I can remember one time when the moon was so bright we could see everything around us as clear as the day. This was a really neat experience. Finally we would go back to the clubhouse around 3:00 AM and go to sleep on our make shift beds. The club house was only a summer event since it did not have insulation and we didn't have an electric heater. During those summer months we found many activities to make up for the limited time we spent in our little club house.

109. The Lawn Mower

There was a very large yard in the front of our house and we cut our lawn with a hand push manual reel mower. It was fairly easy to push as long as the grass was not too long and you kept it moving. We would do our mowing in three sections to keep from fatigue and to give each of my brothers and me a yard to mow. Daddy must have sold a hog or cow because one day he arrived home with a brand new Sears Craftsman gas engine push mower. We couldn't believe what we were seeing. The mower was so easy to use and would cut the grass pushing forward or pulling backward. We all wanted to mow the entire yard until the newness wore off and then we argued again who had the largest yard section to mow. Things just don't change do they?

110. Daddy's California Mystery Trip

I don't recall the year but can remember the event. It was the middle of winter and Daddy announced that he was going to take a trip alone to California to see his brother Wayne. During his time away, there was a vicious snow storm that turned into a blizzard in our area. After the storm was over, nobody was going anywhere. Bob Reigel, a distant neighbor and the owner of the Elevator in Woodington came to our rescue. He knew of Daddy's absence, and Mother not being able to get out for food or supplies. After the blizzard had passed, Bob arrived at our house in a truck suspended 8 feet above the ground on support towers. This vehicle was designed to hover over mature crops for spraying. Bob's truck easily maneuvered over the high snow drifts and he arrived safely to our home.

He brought milk, bread, canned food and heating supplies and would not leave until he was sure we were fully supplied and safe. This was just one example of neighbor helping neighbor during times of need. We came through the storm just fine but we never found out why Daddy took the sudden trip to California. As adults, we even questioned Uncle Wayne about this visit but we never could get a straight answer.

111. Junior The Pig

I can remember many times when the sow would have a litter of pigs. They were cute little animals until they grew up to become a hog. There was one time when one of the little pigs was hanging on to life by a thread. His type was called a runt and many did not live past the first 24 hours. The hope for this one was pretty dim and daddy told us that we could keep him alive by feeding him milk with a baby bottle. He said if he makes it, we could keep him and sell him as a hog at the market. My brothers and I took the challenge and the baby runt pig made it past the critical time period. We then named him Junior. As a little pig, we would play with him and give him extra food. Junior became an adult pig and one day Daddy announced that it was time to take him to the market. We questioned what would happen to Junior and Daddy carefully explained that Junior would become bacon on the plate. This bothered us boys quite a bit. Daddy went on to explain that sooner or later this was the purpose of the pigs and then explained how much money Junior would bring at the market. It didn't take the boys long to make the fatal decision for Junior. Daddy was at work and Mother helped us hook up the trailer to the car and we carted Junior off to the livery stable. The man at the station asked us if we wanted to shoot Junior with his rifle and we quickly declined. I think we received $26.00 to split 3 ways. Junior was a good pig.

112. Kenny Brushing His Teeth

There was something about getting his teeth perfectly clean that was very important to Kenny. He would stand in front the upstairs bathroom mirror and watch the tooth brush move the paste around and around before he would move to the next tooth. Each tooth had to get equal strokes and all surfaces had to be cleaned perfectly. This brought a dilemma when the school bus was waiting in front of the house and all the other Henkaline kids were seated and ready to go. Mother would scream at Kenny to get out there but no motivation would stop him until each tooth had its perfect morning cleansing. Kenny would finish his teeth cleaning ritual and run from the upstairs bathroom to the waiting bus. The bus driver would patiently wait for him, and the kids on the bus were not in any hurry to get to school, so it all worked out just fine.

113. Jerry Was The Athlete - Jack Was Not

Jerry was the athlete of the family. He is left handed, and played most sports. I remember when Jerry and I tried out for a baseball league called "Pony League". The teams met at Ansonia which was about 5 miles from our home. The tryouts were conducted and would separate the ball players into two types of teams. One team would be selected to compete against other teams around the area. The second type was scrub teams that would play among themselves in Ansonia. I remember the best team received red ball caps and the scrub teams received blue ball caps. Jerry made the red team pretty quickly, and I was given a blue cap. As the coaches finalized the selections, I think they noticed that I was holding the blue cap behind my back. After a quick discussion, one of the coaches came over to me and handed me a red cap. I was very pleased. Later I learned that they knew the Henkaline's only had one car and the teams practiced on different days. They felt the only way to get Jerry to play was to draft Jack on the same team. I made the red team but needless to say, I sat the bench the whole season.

114. Food Snacks And Soft Drinks

Our snacks came at night while we watched television. Occasionally, Daddy would buy a wooden case of Coke products at the Woodington Elevator and we would all enjoy a bottle of Coke at night while we watched our favorite television programs. The Coke bottles were made of heavy light transparent green tinted glass and held 6 ounces of liquid. The small bottle of Coke cost 6-cents and the large bottle was 12-cents. This was a real treat for our family and did not come very often. Other snacks consisted of popcorn. We got the popcorn from ears of corn grown in our garden. We would shell the corn and put it in a tin for storage until ready to pop. To pop the corn, we had a heavy metal pan with a stir handle on the top. We would place the correct amount of popcorn in the pan, add grease and put it on the stove burner. This popping process was not something you could just walk away from. When the pan began to heat up and we heard the popping begin we had to stir until all the popcorn kernels were popped. We made several pans to fill the large bowls for the entire family to enjoy. Kool Aid was the drink that came in various flavors. We poured a powder substance from a small Kool Aid envelope and all you had to do was add sugar and water for the quart sized refreshment. Vanilla ice cream with chocolate syrup was also a common snack at night. Sometimes Mother would buy potato chips and we would use a container of sour cream and add onion dip powder to dip the chips. This snack was very rare. Another snack was saltine crackers with a wedge of cheese on top. This was the junk food of our youthful days.

115. The Toilet

One day the well pump quit working and caused some big problems in the Henkaline house. Because there was no water, the upstairs toilet did not work. For the boys it was easy to get around doing "Number One" because the back of the house was secluded from neighbors and all we needed to do was go out the back door and do it on the ground. Doing number two became the challenge during this time. The boys were told the toilet did not work and not to use it but our discipline became weak and the bathroom soon became a raging stink hole. I can remember Kenny walking into the dining room where Mother and Daddy were sitting and announcing the toilet was full. Mother quickly responded, "How can it be full, there is no water." Daddy became very irritated with us for not listening to him and in a loud voice shouted "It is full of what the boys were told not to do, Olive! "Do you understand what I mean?" Mother never said another word and the boys decided to use another method for their bowel movements until the well pump got fixed.

116. Jack - Our Family Doctor

Doctor Kane was our family doctor. He was a medium built, distinguished man with a balding head and a mustache. I remember him being very gentle and kind. He would say, "This is going to bite a little," before giving us a shot. He made several house calls but for the most part we visited his office in Greenville, Ohio. I had a lot of respect for him. He was a good doctor and I think of him as our family friend. There was never a thought of a lawsuit against him or the hospital. There was the understanding that if a person made an honest mistake, it was not anyone's fault, and we would go on with life.

117. Cars Back Then

When I was growing up, the new cars were Ford, Chevy, Oldsmobile, Pontiac, Cadillac, Plymouth, Dodge and Studebaker. That was it. Every year, in the fall, the automobile manufacturers would bring a brand new car design with a dramatic new change from the previous year. We looked forward to seeing the major changes on television, in magazines, or on the road. I think the 1957 Chevy was the best automobile change of my teens. My Uncle Earl Hittle owned a Pontiac / Cadillac Dealership in Greenville and he would drive a new Cadillac every time he visited our home. The white walls were wide and the fins were so high that you would wonder if the car could turn in the wind. The back seat was wide enough for more than three passengers and had more than ample leg room. The flat deck behind the rear seat and back window was long and wide enough for one of us kids to stretch out and sleep during long trips. I slept behind the seat several times in our family car on our trips coming home from Dayton, Ohio. Another sleeping area was the back seat floor. There was a small hump on the floor but not enough to cause a problem. Those were the days of the real car.

Daddy And His Car In The Early Days

118. Daddy's Hat Box

I don't remember the event, but Jerry tells it as a little lesson that Mother gave Daddy. When you went in their bedroom you would find a nice sized walk in closet where you could find a storage place for Mother's and Daddy's clothes. I can remember Daddy had three handsome suits that he wore to church and special formal gatherings. Also the closet had shelves to hold Mother's and Daddy's formal hats. The hats were stored in cardboard hat boxes and placed on the shelves. It turned out that Mother found out that Daddy had some other special uses for one of his hat boxes. She was cleaning out the closet one day when daddy was at work and decided that he had too many dress hats in storage. To her surprise when she opened one of the boxes and removed the hat, she found a sizable amount of cold hard cash that Daddy had hidden away. This made her blazing mad because she was not aware of his secret savings plan. Jerry tells the story that when Daddy arrived home that night Mother casually began discussing her daily activities and dropped the bomb shell that he would not soon forget. She said, "I was cleaning out our closet today and saw that you had several hats stored in boxes you never wear." Carefully describing the box and hat where she found the money she calmly said, "I just took the box and hat along with some other old clothes and threw them out on the fire pile and burned everything." Jerry tells that Dad's face turned pale and he blurted out, "You did what? I had several hundred dollars in the bottom of that box." Mother then said with blazing eyes, "I know that, and I found your private money stash." She went on to explain that she didn't actually burn the box and she never expected Daddy to take money and hide it from her ever again. When his heart began beating again, he agreed to never do that again. Isn't it great when a plan comes together? Score this one for Mother.

119. Breakfast Cereal – Who Needs It?

As a kid, I can't remember eating anything else for breakfast other than Coffee Soup. You say, "Coffee Soup, what's that?" I say, "It's the real deal for the beginning of your day. Cereal is for wimps and drinking coffee at a young age puts hair on your chest, (I am not sure what it does for a girl). The recipe for coffee soup was easy. All you had to do was get a cereal bowl, take crackers and break them into medium size pieces, place sugar over the crackers, then pour coffee with cream over the crackers. But beware. There are two important factors you need to know to get the soup right. First, only use Premium brand crackers (Other brands would allow the coffee to make the crackers soggy and create a mushy substance). Second, don't let the coffee get too hot, because scalding water also will make mushy soup. We used instant coffee from a bottle so all Mother had to do was to put the water in the tea kettle and turn on the stove. Sometimes in the mid-morning, I would get constipated from the coffee, but I thought, "Hey, this is just a little side effect from a great breakfast." I wouldn't even consider another food for breakfast because something else just didn't seem American. I think Mother brain washed us kids because the ingredients were cheap and we could make it on our own with little or no help. We didn't share our little breakfast secret with anybody else at school. We didn't want a cracker shortage in our area.

120. Mother's Apron

I don't think the young people today know what an apron is. The principal use of my mother's apron was to protect her dress underneath because she only had a few. Her apron was also used because it was easier to wash aprons than dresses, and aprons used less material. The apron was made from a pattern purchased from a department store. Those big pockets could carry anything from recipes' to spice jars for food cooking. But along with that, it served as a potholder for removing hot pans from the stove. It was wonderful for drying tears and on occasion was even used for cleaning out dirty ears. From our chicken coop, the apron was used for carrying eggs, and fussy chicks. When the weather was cold Mother would wrap it around her arms. Those big old aprons wiped many a perspiring brow, bent over the hot kitchen stove. From the garden, it carried all sorts of vegetables. After the peas had been shelled, it sometimes carried out the hulls. In the fall, the apron was used to bring in apples that had fallen from the trees. When unexpected company drove up the driveway it was surprising how much furniture that old apron could dust in a matter of seconds. It will be a long time before someone invents something that will replace that 'old-time apron' that served so many purposes. Today's health department would go crazy trying to figure out how many germs were on that old apron but I don't think any of the Henkaline kids ever caught anything but love from Mother's apron.

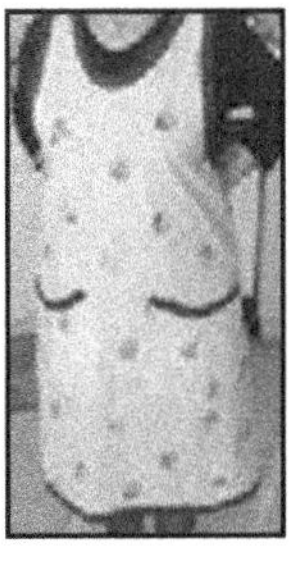

121. What Are Rivvels?

When we were growing up Mother made a wonderful soup dish that we called rivvels. The Henkaline kids were very pleased when the bowl of rivvles appeared on our dinner table. Since rivvels was a common dish at the Henkaline house we thought everybody knew about them. After we were married, I asked Sharon if she could make a bowl of rivvles and she told me that she never heard of them. Being stationed in Berlin, Germany I asked our military friends about rivvels and they gave the same answer, "What are rivvels?" I tried to explain what they looked like and how they tasted, but nobody understood the rivvel soup. To my surprise, it appeared like the Henkaline's were the only humans that ever heard of rivvels. It was a delight to me when Sharon finally found the rivvles recipe in a popular cookbook. This recipe has been entered below so you can have the wonderful rivvels soup dish that the Henkaline kids enjoyed on Hathaway Road.

Potato Rivvel Soup
3lb. potatoes, peeled and cubed
½ cup onion
Pinch of salt
2 T. butter
Salt and pepper
1 cup milk
1 cup water
Rivvels (recipe follows)

Put potatoes and onions in a large kettle with water to barely cover and pinch of salt and cook until the potatoes are done. Do not drain the water. Take a potato masher and mash the potatoes in the water until they are roughly mashed. There will still be small lumps. Then add the butter and salt and pepper to taste.

Next, add the liquid – you will need to use a combination of milk and water because the milk gives the soup a creamy richness. Bring the soup to a gentle bubbling simmer. Now make the rivvles.

Rivvels

1 cup flour
1 egg
½ tsp. salt

In a medium bowl, mix the flour and salt. Break the egg into the flour mixture and mix together until you have lumps about the size of grapes. This is a fairly messy process, so feel free to use your hands to mix. Drop these rivvles into the soup and, stirring occasionally, cook them until done, about 10 minutes or so depending on their size. If the soup is too thick, you can add more milk. Adjust the seasoning to taste before serving.

122. Pear Pie

It all started one day when the pear tree in front of our house began dropping its fruit onto the ground. Daddy saw the fruit and asked Mother if she could make a pear pie. Mother quickly replied that pears were not something that would make a good pie but Daddy insisted that he would like her to give it a try. A couple of days later the pear pie arrived at the dinner table. The pie looked great with a rich crust covering the dish but when we cut into the pie we found the pears were a soft mushy pear substance with little taste. Daddy ate his first and last pear pie. He also learned that Mother was right and never requested another pear pie.

123. Daddy Adjusting The Mirror

Daddy had a ritual about adjusting the interior rear view mirror before moving the car one inch. He would sit behind the steering wheel, look at the mirror, tap it with his index finger up or down and then tap it again to the right or left. Sometimes he would over tap in one direction and be required to tap it back towards center. I never understood why he just didn't move his head and leave the mirror alone. I wanted to ask the question, but I understood that mirror tapping was important to Daddy.

124. A Visit From Cousin Dennis

It was a typical summer day and the boys were outside playing in the yard. To our surprise, we saw our cousin Dennis Hittle ride in our yard on his bicycle. Dennis was our first cousin and the son of Francis and Mary Hittle. His Daddy was the brother to our Mother. Dennis lived in Greenville and he said he made the 10 mile journey to spend a couple of days with his Aunt Ollie, Uncle Bill and the Henkaline kids. We were delighted to see him and pleased that he was going to spend some time with us. Dennis was older and was looked up to by my brothers and me for some very special reasons.

Dennis lived in the city of Greenville, Ohio and to us country boys, we thought he was from "The Big City." Another reason that we looked up to Dennis was that he was always getting into mischief and didn't seem to be afraid of anything or anybody. One story he told us was the time when he and his buddies ran beside the Greenville Police office and threw lighted fire crackers in the open windows. We couldn't believe our ears as he gave us the details. Another story was when he and his friends put soap powder in the town center water fountain. This huge water fountain was in the middle of a beautiful grassed circle located at the center of Greenville's Main Street. The circle and fountain was known as a landmark of Greenville and the entrance to the beautiful downtown area. After the box of soap powder was thrown in, the water became a mountain of suds that lasted for days. Anita tells us that during any church service she remembers that if a door opened at any time or any location of the sanctuary, cousin Dennis would most likely be the one walking through. This brave and bold cousin made us admire and envy his character. I don't recall what all we did during his short visit but I know we had fun with "Dennis The Great."

125. Sunday Trips To Uncle Henry's

Some Sundays we would take a trip to Dayton, Ohio to visit Uncle Henry and Aunt Della Buser. Aunt Della was my mother's sister. Uncle Henry was a short bullish man with a bark that would stop a drunk. On the other hand Aunt Della was a meek, well mannered, frail woman who just smiled a lot and let Uncle Henry verbally abuse her and anybody else in his way. The other side of Uncle Henry was that he was very generous and had a heart of gold. He would do anything in his power to help others in need.

These trips to Uncle Henry's house were kind of boring to the boys because there were no kids to play with in his neighborhood. To entertain ourselves, we would watch his television or go down to his basement to explore what our uncle had in storage. What we found down there were lots of tools and items that were of the same type and kind. My brothers and I suspected that either Uncle Henry liked to purchase many duplicate items or that he was robbing his company blind where he worked. We never challenged him to what we saw. Our boredom quickly vanished when we found his walls papered with posters of naked girls. I personally would rather read the advertisement script on the posters and admire the vivid color of the posters but many times my eyes would drift up to the girls. I clearly remember that Jerry and Kenny were looking at those girls with wild thoughts entering their minds. We couldn't stay all afternoon in the basement because we were afraid somebody upstairs might catch on and come down to see what we were doing. We just stayed long enough to get our nudity appetite filled and return to the living room to watch more television. Sometimes we would sneak back down for another quick look before the long drive home. We really loved our Uncle Henry and his interest in collecting beautiful wall posters.

In the early days Uncle Henry had two small boxer terrier dogs that were black and white with bulging eyes. We never liked those dogs because they would nip at us when we tried to pet them. Uncle Henry loved his dogs with a passion and treated them like kings. We learned that when Aunt Della called him at work one day to inform that one of his dogs died he cried like a baby. When the second dog died he never replaced them. We were glad because we didn't like to be around a nipping dog. At the time, I never understood Uncle Henry's emotion for his dogs until I became an adult and my own dog died. I cried just like my Uncle Henry.

The Sunday visit to Uncle Henry's and Aunt Della's was always the same. We would arrive in the afternoon to visit, have dinner and leave early in the evening to go home. I remember one time late in the afternoon, Daddy, Uncle Henry and boys were watching television in the living room and the ladies were in the kitchen preparing the evening meal.

Uncle Henry was sitting in his favorite recliner with his legs and feet in the horizontal position. Daddy was sitting in a swivel chair and the boys were lying on the floor. All of a sudden Uncle Henry yells out, "*Della get in here!*" The boys were very much alarmed at this outburst and froze into position to see what was coming next. We saw Aunt Della come trotting in from the kitchen to see what Uncle Henry wanted. As she approached the chair, Uncle Henry pointed down at his feet and said, "Reach down there and pull my socks from between my toes." The boys made a mental note of this technique to use on our future wives at a future date but later learned that only Uncle Henry could get by with such a command.

126. Mocking Uncle Henry

My brothers and I were never accused of not frequently testing our uncle's short temper. On one occasion we were lying on his living room floor and began to playfully mock everything he said. He avoided us as long as he could then let out in an unexplainable voice, "I'm going to ram my fist down the next one of you who mocks me." I was quick to notice that my two brothers and I kept our mouths shut for the remainder of the visit. I was afraid to even talk to anybody, thinking that I might say something that Uncle Henry might have said earlier and I didn't remember it. We got out of his house with his fist not touching our mouths so we felt pretty lucky that day.

127. Uncle Henry Locked Out Of Our Car

Daddy, Uncle Henry and the boys drove to my Grandmother Henkaline's house one summer day. I can't remember what we did to our dear Uncle Henry but we really set his temper off to the maximum. We were outside and Daddy wasn't near the event. We really set him off and Uncle Henry was so mad at us that he began chasing us. All three of us ran to the car parked in the driveway and locked all the doors. Uncle Henry came steaming up to the car like a raving maniac and screamed "Unlock this car door right now!" Without saying a word, all three of the boys just looked straight ahead and shook their head "No" in unison as we set in the frozen position. It didn't take a mental giant for us to understand the door locks were our best option in our current situation. He finally walked away muttering something. Later Daddy came back with him and chewed us out to settle him down so we could go home. We learned later, that cousin Dennis Hittle had a few similar moments with Uncle Henry.

128. Uncle Henry As Santa Claus

Our Uncle Henry was a gruff man, but we all knew he had a heart of gold. He would give us nice gifts, and then in his gruff voice say, "Now don't break that or I will box your ears." In my younger years he even came to the Hathaway house as Santa Claus. He purchased an expensive Santa outfit to entertain the kids in his church and us Henkaline kids too. We knew he was not Santa, but it was fun to have him visit us. We had some wonderful times with our Uncle Henry and Aunt Della. They were very wonderful people who were generous to us and we loved them very much. We all agreed that our Uncle Henry Buser was a diamond in the rough, and I think he loved us too.

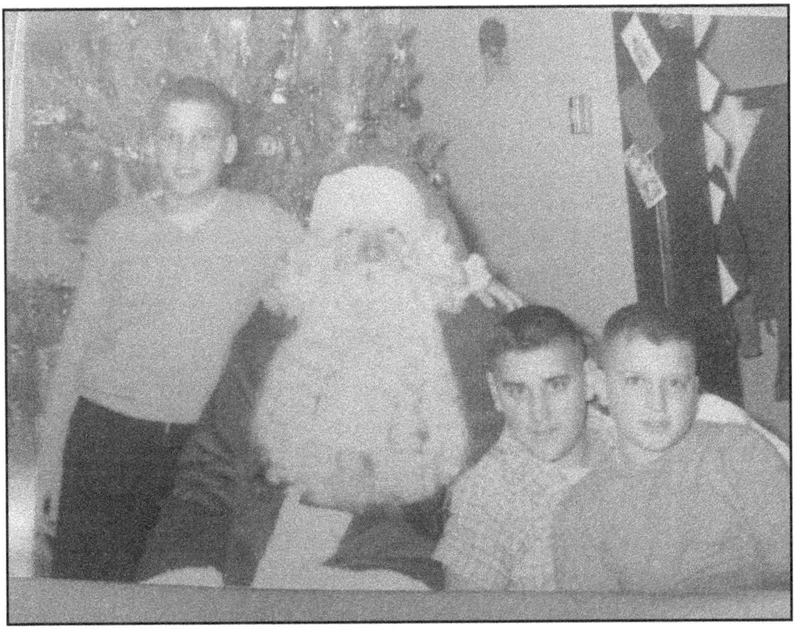

Uncle Henry With The Boys At Christmas Time On Hathaway Road

129. Visiting Our Aunts

My Aunt Ethel and Aunt Carrie lived together in Greenville, Ohio. The house was owned by Aunt Ethel and she rented the upstairs out to single adults for extra income. She invited Aunt Carrie to live with her in the downstairs. They both were sisters of my mother and had lost their husbands. Aunt Ethel was a refined woman and wore a lot of make up, plenty of expensive jewelry and a mink coat when she went out on special occasions. She laughed a lot and took everything in stride. Aunt Carrie was more serious with no sense of humor, wore plain clothes and wanted everybody and everything to be in proper order. Their different personalities did not hinder their relationship and they both seemed happy to be together. There were some Thanksgiving holidays when the two aunts would invite the Hittle families over for lunch and afternoon visits. I remember their home was small and it became very crowded when the adults and children visited. They only had one bathroom and this became a big problem if the large plates of food eaten at the lunch table began working on the digestive system.

My biggest memory of these two aunts was that they were hooked on the daily television soap operas, "*The Guiding Light*", "*All My Children*" and "*As The World Turns.*" When we visited, they would describe the events of their beloved characters on television and recite the happenings from the previous days show. It seemed like they lived within the story script and they would become very emotional when happiness or tragedy struck their friends in the Hollywood dramas. We visited their home one afternoon when we saw both huddled in front of their television. Their eyes froze to the happenings of the day and we dare not interrupt or say a word as they gasped, wept, hissed or laughed out loud with pure joy of the drama happening before their very eyes. I wanted to tell them this was just a television drama but I loved them very much and did not want to place them in shock and affect their mental health.

130 My School Days In The Hallway

I was a little ornery when I was in the 7th grade and often the teacher would get enough of me being a nuisance and send me out of the class to stand in the hallway. I really didn't care about this punishment because I didn't have a burning desire to learn what she was teaching. The question while out there was what to do and how to avoid being caught by the principal. I knew if he found me there I would be taken to his office and might get the paddle to my bottom. To solve this little dilemma I would hover over the Encyclopedia set that was located just outside my classroom. If the principal happened to come around, I would have a book open and act like I was doing individual research. This was a great plan and I never got caught by the principal. Sharon Brown, who later became my wife, told me that if she had to leave her class early or go to the bathroom, she would expect to see me in the hallway.

131. The Little Tithe Jar

The folks were faithful believers in tithing and gave the first 10% of their money back to God. The tithe money was cash put in a large jelly jar that was kept in the china cabinet located in the dining room. The china cabinet drawer was never locked and the jar was not hidden. Anybody in the family could open the jar and find several hundred dollars at any time. As the boys got older and began to go out on Saturday nights, we sometimes needed a little cash loan to get us by until we worked for more money. Daddy would allow us to borrow from the tithe jar as long as we placed an IOU paper showing the amount of money borrowed and who borrowed the money. There was never a time limit to pay back and no interest on the loan. This was an honor system and we knew that it was cheating God if we misused this privilege. I think Daddy wanted to teach us a lesson in honesty and respect for God's money by allowing us to do this. We always paid back every penny we took. Daddy may have reviewed the IOU's, but he never said a word about the amount and repayment plan. I think this was a good honesty lesson to teach his kids.

132. The Family Income

I don't ever remember having any family conversations about the money my parents earned or the family budget, while I was growing up. Daddy worked in a factory and his salary was not what you would call above average. Mother's job was to manage the home by contributing with her talent of cooking efficient meals, cleaning the house, washing our clothes, sewing and helping with the livestock to name a few. What they budgeted as a team always met our needs. We were taught to not waste anything and we didn't dream of spending money on luxury items. The only exception I can recall was when we traveled to California on vacation. Our other vacations were short and simple and some years we didn't go on vacation but rather did things in our area. We had plenty of the basic essentials and always enjoyed plenty of food on the table. The boys wore their brothers "hand-me-down" clothes and new clothes usually came once a year during the Greenville Dollar Days sales event. Our new clothes came just before the new school year began. A lack of money never surfaced and the kids never worried about not having what we needed. I think their secret was that my parents never borrowed money for anything other than the farm we called home. When it was time to purchase a new car, Daddy got out his quarters and half dollar coin collection and took them with him along with a bank check to purchase the car. I think that Daddy felt that showing actual cash when making the car purchase gave him an edge to make the best deal. Savings was always part of the weekly budgeting and an additional Christmas savings account was always in place. Every Friday was pay day and that night Daddy would sit at the dining room table and complete his financial book work. The cash that he did not deposit in the bank during his lunch hour on pay day was brought home for general usage. The tithe jar always received the first amount of cash for Church and God's work. When the farm was paid off, the general savings plan was accelerated to bridge any financial needs or unexpected expenses. Bible financial practices were firmly in place and I think the Henkaline house practices were the core reason for our family's financial success.

133. Our Baseball Field

We played a lot of baseball in a pasture field just south of our house when I was a kid. I remember we tried to improve our baseball diamond by trying to use a shovel to remove the grass and top soil and carve out the base lines. When we reached half way to first base, we quickly learned this was more work than it was worth so we went back to the imaginary lines to each base pad. There was no home plate back fence to stop the pitched ball, but the field served us well with plenty of space on the sides and in the outfield. We had bats, gloves and several hard baseballs to play the game and many neighborhood kids had a lot of fun on our make shift baseball field.

134. The Baseball Game That Went Stupid

One Sunday we decided to play baseball by hitting a wiffle ball in the front yard. The makeshift bases were set up and the game began. We found the wiffle would not travel past the infield so I decided to make the game more interesting by substituting the wiffle ball with our basketball. Since this was my idea, I demanded to be the first batter. When Jerry tossed the basketball to me, I used all my strength to hit it with my bat. As I swung at the ball I anticipated an "out of the park" celebration, but instead the bat hit the ball and bounced back and struck me just above my eye. I was dazed at first then felt the blood running down my face. Another trip to the doctor and three stitches later, I was back in action. Then, to my dismay, the basketball didn't even go as far as the wiffle ball. At the time I did not understand inertia properties, but I quickly learned that if you don't think before you act; stupid things can happen to you.

135. The Meat In The Freezer

Daddy would raise cattle and pigs on the farm each year to butcher meat for the family. I remember taking the cow or pig to the slaughter house and return a week later to pick up the wax paper packages of frozen meat. Each package was marked with what kind of meat it contained. The majority of packages were marked "Hamburger". There were also packages of liver and some steaks, but 85% of the packages were always marked hamburger. The story behind this was that even choice parts to the beef were ground into hamburger because it was the boy's favorite meat and an easy meal for Mother to fix. I recall the butcher questioning Daddy about grinding choice cuts into hamburger but his instructions were always to make the majority of meat into hamburger. I think we had the best tasting hamburgers in our part of the country.

136. Daddy's Journal

Daddy kept a journal for keeping track of all his purchases. I remember many Friday night's seeing him sit at the dining room table as he logged his purchases. I took the time as an adult to review his journal book and understand about his attention to detail. Daddy's journal shows entries of every item he purchased which includes the price and dates for items such as screws and washers at 1 cent each to large equipment purchases. The journal is a very interesting book to review. Jerry received the original book and we received a copy.

137. Selling The Kitchen Range

It was decided that Mother would get a new Hotpoint range for cooking. In those days we just didn't throw the old one out but rather would sell it to a used appliance store. I remember a man named Mr. Cruise came to our house on Saturday morning to look at the old range that we had for sale. Mother timed the event perfectly and had an apple and cherry pie coming out of the oven when he came into the kitchen. The fresh pie aroma filled the room and the range was purchased on the spot. I think we got $20.00 for it. Now I know where I inherited my sales skills.

138. The Ice Storm

One cold winter time when I was around 11 years old we experienced a severe ice storm. Heavy ice froze to the tree limbs and electric lines and caused telephone and power lines to break. We were without electricity in our house for about four days. Daddy was able to go to work but schools were closed. We had to find another source for heat and light inside the house. We owned a little white porcelain coal oil stove and it was brought into the kitchen. The kitchen was one of the smallest rooms in the house so we closed all the doors to maintain the heat in the room and keep us warm. Kerosene lamps provided the light when needed. I remember that Jerry's friend John Herron came to the house during this storm and stayed with us in our little kitchen shelter. Jerry got out the playing cards and we had fun playing a marathon of different card games. Mother even joined in on several of the games. We had a great time entertaining ourselves and this event brings cherished memories back to my mind.

139. Television Stations

It may be hard to understand in this day and age but when I grew up we had only three television stations. They were ABC, NBC and CBS. The reception for all three were turned on in the morning and shut off around midnight. During this shut down time you would see a stationary single image and hear a medium pitch sound.

During the morning you would find game shows like "*The Price Is Right*" hosted by Bob Barker. Also "*Captain Kangaroo*" and "Mr. Rogers" would be there for the kids. Around 1:00 pm. the soaps would begin. Some titles I remember were "*The Guiding Light*" and "*All My Children*". Mother never got hooked on the soaps but Aunt Ethel and Aunt Carrie seemed to live for the events. After school were shows called "*Bozo The Clown*" and the "*Mickey Mouse Show.*" Week nights we watched the shows "*Raw Hide*", "*The Rifleman*", and "*Wagon Train.*" On Friday night came "*Outer Limits*", and "*The Twilight Zone.*" Saturday mornings were reserved for the kids to see "*Bullwinkle*" and lots of cartoons. Saturday night was the premier of television. Around 7:00 came "77 *Sunset Strip*", "*The Lawrence Welk Show*" and the grand finale was "*Gunsmoke.*" *Lawrence Welk* was Daddy's favorite. We tolerated this show because there was not much else to do and we knew *Gunsmoke* would follow. Those were great times to watch television as a family.

140. Our Television Set

Back in the late 1950's and 1960's, a television was an important part of the household treasures. The television box was made of real wood and had a 17" black and white screen to view. When we turned on the television, it took a few minutes before a picture arrived to the screen. The inside of the set was filled with tubes, transistors, resisters, circuit boards and many wires. The front panel consisted of an off/on switch, a channel selector and a dial to tune in the frequency for a better picture. On the back side of the television, you found knobs to adjust for brightness, contrast, up/down and side to side picture alignment on the screen. There was no remote control to do anything. A person had to manually tune the volume and station. We couldn't even dream of what a remote could do and we would have thought a person would be insane to pay for television viewing. The antenna wire was flat and had two leads attached to a pole antenna positioned high on the side of our house. When a storm was coming, we shut off the TV set and disconnected the antenna wire and electrical plug. We were told that lightning could strike the antenna or give an electrical surge that would ruin our set. This was a big thing because we only owned one television set and it was expensive. We wanted to keep it in perfect condition for our entertainment.

141. Television Repair

A dreaded day was when the television set quit working. I remember several times when this occurred. Dad knew a television repairman in Greenville named Andy Arnett. He was a crippled man but knew his stuff. We begged our Dad to get the broken TV to Andy as fast as he could when it quit working. I remember that we would load the television in the car trunk and head to Greenville. The television was pretty heavy, but we carried it to the repair shop located in the back of Andy's house. We would sit it on a big counter and Andy would take the back panel off the set to determine what was wrong. We could see the many tubes glowing and Andy had a tester that could determine what was wrong. The boys would watch the process in amazement and cross our fingers that Andy would have the replacement tube or resistor to send the set back with us the same night. A bad picture tube was not good news but something Andy could order, if needed. On most occasions we would have to leave the set and it would take between one and two weeks for Andy to get the tubes and have the time to repair our set. It never entered anybody's mind that a household would have more than one television set. Those were long nights during the wait to get our television set back.

142. Buying The Television

Different television manufacturing companies had similar control options but the front adjustment knobs and the cabinet style varied. This was important, but the most important element between each television manufacturer was the clarity of the picture. The only way to evaluate this was to compare the television sets side by side. Daddy would call three furniture companies to deliver their television model for a trial review. He would allow two to set beside each to compare for the best features and best picture. The loser of the two would be returned and the third set would come to compete against the winning set. The store owners knew the trial process and hoped their set would be the winner. Our whole family would participate in the vote for the best features and the best picture of the televisions on trial. The two step trial period took about a week and it was an exciting time for us. In the end we all agreed on the set to keep and felt ownership choosing the winner.

143. The New Radio

Before my teens, radio stations were only received on AM frequency. The new FM channels arrived and brought a new variety of channels and better local reception. Mother wanted to listen to local Christian stations and one Saturday, Daddy took us to a furniture store to purchase the new radio (shown in the picture below). This radio was another center of entertainment and was placed on the television set for our listening enjoyment.

Jack In The Mid 60's With Our Television Set And Radio In The Background

144. The Telephone

The one and only telephone in our house was located on a wall in our dining room. It was about waist high and we had a chair to sit on while using the phone. I can remember the earliest version as a black angled box with a speak/hear receiver cradled on the top. There was no dial feature so you were required to lift the receiver and wait for an operator to answer for your instructions to make a call. She would identify herself as the operator and ask the caller what number they wanted to call. She would connect the two phones and the other telephone would ring. When the other party answered the operator would leave the line and you would have approximately seven minutes to talk before being disconnected. Later we received an updated version with a number dial. This allowed us to dial the number we wanted to call. An operator was not needed unless you wanted to make a long distance call which required dialing "0".

Our telephone was on a Party Line. This meant that others in your neighborhood could pick up their receiver and listen to your conversation. You didn't know who they were but you knew they were there because of a click in and out. If you picked up the receiver and heard a dial tone, you were able to make your call. If somebody else on your party line was using the phone, you had to wait until they finished. The seven minute time limit for all calls was still in effect so nobody could dominate the party line.

I began to frequently use our telephone in my teens after falling in love with Sharon Brown. I would call her every evening and we would spend up to a ½ hour or longer on the phone. We got around the "Cut Off" device by quickly hanging up after we were cut off and redialing before anybody else on our party line entered the line. Others would listen to our conversation, but we didn't care and continued talking. Once in a while we would hear somebody say, "Get off the line, and let somebody else use it," but that didn't stop us from our lengthy calls because "We Were In Love."

The Telephone

145. Shopping For Food

We went shopping for our food at the A&P grocery store in Greenville, Ohio. This was a family event and usually happened on Friday night. The shopping sometimes became a social event because my parents would sometimes see friends there and chat for awhile in the aisles at the store. The large grocery cart we used became completely full when we reached the check out and the register would go no higher than $25.00. There was no such thing as a credit card so cash or check was the only method for payment. I remember one time at the grocery store, when we were ready to check out, Daddy found that he had left his wallet and checkbook at home. He quickly found a friend he had been talking to in the aisle and borrowed $20.00 until the next day. In those days, the only credit you had available was to go to a bank and borrow for a car or borrow for your house. All other purchases were cash only.

146. Churning For Butter

Our cows provided our milk and butter for our family. Mother pasteurized the milk before we were allowed to drink it. She took the cream from off the top of the milk and saved it for making butter. The cream was put into a butter churn that required her to pump the handle up and down until the cream turned into butter. She then took the butter and formed it into a paddy that looked like the shell of a turtle. We did not know it at the time, but the real butter we ate each meal was a delicacy in many other homes. Jane Snyder, who was our neighbor, asked Daddy if he would sell her some butter for their table. It was then when we learned our butter was taken for granted.

147. Just Shut Your Eyes

I can remember there were times when we were faced with a high dollar item to purchase. Daddy would spend time to determine if we really needed to buy the expensive item. If he felt we really needed it, he would state, "I am just going to shut my eyes and buy it." He never went back on questioning his decision. His way of processing the purchase decision and making up his mind to purchase was effective. He justified the purchase and paid for it by "Shutting his eyes and doing it."

148. Ice Skating

When Kenny and I were around ten and twelve years old, we took up ice skating. Mother heard about a lady in Greenville who had two sets of used skates and she took us to her home to look at them. They were like new and we purchased them that night. Kenny learned to skate first and I followed soon afterwards. There was a pond along the railroad tracks near Woodington and we would meet Terry Shiverdecker to go skating. We weren't great skaters, but it was a fun thing to do during the cold winter months. My parents were good about purchasing reasonable things to make us happy.

149. Kenny's Moped

When Kenny was about 12 years old, he saved enough money to buy a used Moped. This was a bicycle type vehicle with pedals and a small motor. The pedals were used to start the motor or you could use them like a bicycle. The law stated that you had to be 15 to ride the Moped so Kenny would peddle it when he felt a highway patrolman was near. One day, he decided to remove the motor, tear it down into parts and paint the frame. He had the moped parts and the motor completely in pieces lying in sections and in sequence on the garage floor. The family guessed that he would never get it running again. To our surprise he replaced all the worn parts, painted the frame gold and re-assembled it back together in running condition. Kenny had a mechanical mind that impressed the entire family.

The Christmas Santa and Reindeer Set

150. The Christmas Reindeer

Daddy found the Santa and Reindeer at G. C. Murphy's during his Friday lunch hour visit to pick up candy. The reindeer were made of beautiful porcelain with large bright eyes. They had silver antlers and colored ornaments around their mid section. Some of the reindeer bodies were light brown and others were dark brown. He began buying them the middle of November one year and they came to our house very slowly because Daddy bought them in quantities of two per week. Santa and the sleigh were finally purchased and the complete set was ready for our Christmas display just before Christmas. I think each reindeer was purchased for around $2.00. The set was placed on top of the piano with a white cotton base to represent snow, and Christmas lights surrounded the set. A few years later our reindeer display was jeopardized when the small Christmas lights became so hot they caught the cotton on fire. Daddy quickly took the burning cotton and threw it out the front door. During the removal of the burning cotton, one reindeer fell off the piano to the floor and was completely broken and could not be repaired. Another reindeer fell and broke but we were able to glue and repair it. The glued reindeer remained in the set but was in very poor condition. Daddy tried to replace both reindeer but he found they were no longer available for sale so the reindeer set that continued to be displayed but was never complete in future seasons.

151. A 2010 Reindeer Update

After both Daddy and Mother passed away the incomplete reindeer set was given to our son Chris by the Henkaline family. Sharon and I made it our mission to look for a replacement for the two reindeer. In 1984, we took a picture of one reindeer and placed a "Wanted" advertisement" in the Greenville newspaper. It was our hope that somebody else in the Greenville area had also purchased the reindeer and would be willing to sell theirs to us. We agreed that were willing to pay a very high price to anyone willing to sell. The advertisement received no response. Our next plan was to visit antique stores and inquire to the owner about our search. As I traveled in my work I frequently visited antique stores all over the mid-west. I searched for over 40 years with no luck. When Sharon and I went to antique stores we always looked through the Christmas decoration sections for our reindeer. An old man who owned an antique store once stated, "You will find the reindeer at a time when you are not looking for them." I tucked his prediction away and hoped it would come true.

It was October of 2010 when Sharon and I decided to go to Kendallville, Indiana to visit their annual Apple Festival. We invited our friends John and Beth Cook to go along and we anticipated a great time. The Kendallville Fair Grounds had many exhibits of musical entertainment, many varieties of food, crafts and antiques. One of the many large buildings was full of many antique displays. John and I were about twenty feet ahead of Sharon and Beth as we walked down the long aisle. All of a sudden, Sharon yelled for me to quickly come back to her. She took me to a booth that I had already passed and showed me two perfect matched reindeer in the back of one booth. She later told me that as she and Beth passed the booth, she saw a lady holding one of the reindeer in her hand to examine for purchase. When the lady put the reindeer down Sharon was on the run to get me. We went back into the booth and I grabbed both reindeer at once so nobody else could have them. They came with a cheap wooden sleigh and a worn out stuffed Santa Claus. Expecting a very high price I asked the owner how much she wanted for the set. Before she answered, I told her that I was not really interested in the Santa or the sleigh. She went on to explain that she got them from an estate sale where an old man had purchased them many years before. She finally said she wanted $12.00 for the entire set. I couldn't pay her fast enough. It was later that I remembered that old antique dealer was right. We found them when we were least expecting it.

When we got them home, we decided to put them away and give our reindeer treasures to Chris and Laura for Christmas. We asked them over before Christmas to present our find. When Chris opened the box and saw what was inside, his eyes went wide open and he kept saying, "I can't believe you found them." He told us that he had also been searching many years and had searched the internet several times with no luck. He said that each year his kids would fight each other to see who got to set up the reindeer display over his fireplace at his home. After he left and later that day, he called us back to tell us the reindeers were the best Christmas present we ever gave him. The amazing part of this story is that it took over forty years to find the reindeer replacements. We needed two reindeer. God provided us with just those two. We trust that some day one of our grandchildren will pass this story on to their children as they display the complete set at Christmas.

152. The Boys' Favorite Christmas

We had some very ragged used bicycles when I was a child. Mine was an old black beater that was too large and I had to climb on the outside concrete steps to get on it. One fall afternoon Daddy announced that he was going to take our bikes to a repair shop and have them painted and fully repaired. He added icing to his story by saying, "You boys need good bikes to ride." I thought this was a great idea and we fell for his story. I asked for my black beauty to be painted shinny gold. As the weeks went by, I complained that I wanted my bike back because it was taking too long to get the work complete. Daddy gave some excuse and quickly changed the subject.

Christmas Eve finally arrived and around 7:00 pm mother announced that the boys were to follow Anita upstairs before we were allowed to open our presents. We didn't know why, but we understood that when the giver of gifts makes a request, we had better listen. We waited for what seemed forever in the cold upstairs bedroom. Anita warned that if we went downstairs early we would not receive any presents that year. We argued that all they had to do was transport our presents from storage to the tree and it shouldn't take this long. We heard noises but nobody talking from the first floor.

Mother finally made the announcement to come down. I think Jerry went first, followed by Kenny and then me. When we rounded the corner at the bottom of the steps we were greeted in the living room with three shiny new Schwinn bicycles. We couldn't believe our eyes. The bicycles were the same model but in colors; green and white, red and white and black and white. Jerry ran for the green one, Ken grabbed the red and I couldn't wait to get my hands on the black and white one. They were the most beautiful Christmas presents we had ever received. We wanted to take a ride immediately, but it was dark and snow was on the ground. Instead we just hovered over them, sat on them and dreamed of the ride in the morning. What we didn't know until that night, was that Daddy had traded our old bicycles in for new ones and during our wait that Christmas Eve night, and it took Daddy and Mother some time to transport the three new bikes from our neighbor's barn to our living room. We learned later that the bikes had been stored for some time in Emmitt Welch's barn. The folks were worried that we would all want the same color but to their amazement we each ran to the color of our first choice. Not fighting over the color of our bicycles made that Christmas even more perfect. I know that Mother and Daddy sacrificed a lot to get us those bikes and this story has been told many times over the years as a tribute to their unselfish love for us.

153. The Christmas Decorations

I remember when I was very young, we always had a fresh-cut Christmas tree with many colorful decorations and large colored bulbs. We put the final touches on the tree by loading it down with silver icicles and lots of angel hair which looked like white spider webs all over the tree. We decorated the piano with the reindeer and had a white lighted "Frosty The Snowman" placed on the television.

To add to our Christmas decorations I remember taking a window cleaner called Glass Wax and dabbing it with a sponge over a stencil snowflake, candy cane, or Santa Claus. It came out of the can as a pink wax. When it dried, it left a white paste on the glass in the cut-out area of the stencil. If you didn't like it, all you had to do was wipe it off and start over again. When the Christmas season was over you could add more paste and clean the entire window.

In my middle teens my parents bought a silver tree with a revolving colored disk light to change the color of the tree. I think Mother and Daddy thought it was the modern thing to do and much safer and easier to decorate. This silver tree lasted for several years until the artificial green evergreen hit the market. From that time on we decorated a tree that resembled the real thing.

154. Going To Church On Sunday

We attended church service most every Sunday morning at the Christian and Missionary Alliance Church in Greenville, Ohio. I can clearly remember going to a Sunday school class that built my basic knowledge of the Bible teachings. After Sunday School we went into the worship service where we would squirm around in our seats while the pastor gave his message to the adults. There were no gyms to play ball and no outside uses for our church in those days. The church was a place to worship and our religion was taken very seriously. We sometimes attended the Sunday night services. Sunday evening was also a time to watch Walt Disney on television. Just about the time the show became interesting was when we had to leave for the evening church service. Mother would tell us to turn off the television and get in the car. It was very discouraging, but we knew that we were going and had no other choice. At the time I thought, "Wouldn't it be great if somebody would invent a way to get the sound of the television on our car radio so at least we could hear what was going on." Little did I know what the future of electronics would bring.

On several occasions, Daddy would announce that he was not going to attend the service on a Sunday night. The boys would beg to stay home and sometimes we were allowed to skip the evening service and stay home with Daddy. After mother left, he would say that we were going to have a party and would cut cheese slices and put them on crackers for a snack. We would eat while we watched television and told him that his party was a great idea. Secretly we didn't care what he called it, we just knew we were fed snacks and we didn't have to go to Sunday night church.

155. The Revival

The Christian and Missionary Alliance Church occasionally had a week long revival service. I think I was about 12 years old when Reverend Bill Weston came to our church to conduct the revival. He was a "Hell, Fire and Damnation" type of speaker who could scare the pants off you. He could go from getting tears to getting fears from the congregation. He convinced us that if we did not confess our sins and give our life to Jesus Christ, we were going straight to Hell. It was in one of these meetings that I went to the altar for the first time and asked Jesus Christ to come into my life. Kenny and Jerry did the same during his visit. I will never forget Bill Weston and I am grateful that he was a part of my initial walk with the Lord.

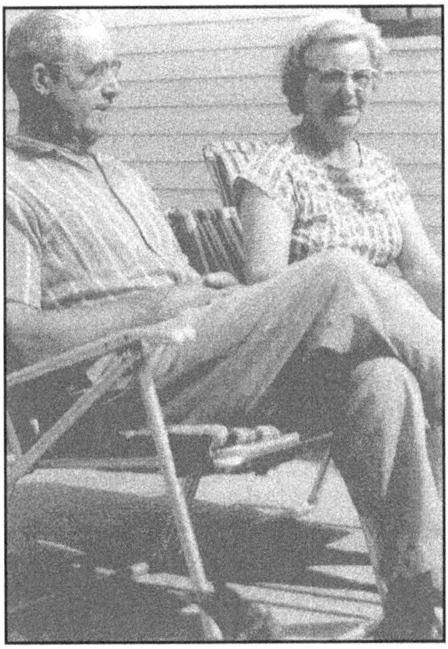

Mother and Daddy Relaxing On The Back Patio On A Sunday Afternoon

156. Fried Chicken

A popular Sunday lunch was fried chicken. It was as fresh as you could get because the chicken on our table was alive and walking around the day before. On Saturday morning Mother would select the victim. The death for the chicken was not an easy one. Mother would hold the chicken by the legs and in one quick sweep; step down hard on its head to the ground and pull hard. This would remove the head and leave a bloody stem at the neck. It was then time to release the legs and allow the chicken to flop around the yard until death set in. After the flopping stopped, Mother would collect the carcass and take it to the kitchen where boiling water was waiting. The chicken would be placed in the boiling water until the feathers could easily be removed. After this she would use a sharp kitchen knife to scrape the outer skin and remove any feather points that remained. Next it was time to cut open the carcass and remove the unwanted inner parts. She then would cut the remaining legs, wings, breast, liver, gizzards, and neck into pieces and place them in a large bowl for frying the next day. On Sunday after church, she would put a little flour and seasoning on the parts and place them in the frying pan. The previous day's gruesome sight would quickly be forgotten as we all sat around the Sunday dinner table and ate the fresh delicious fried chicken.

157. The Automobile Joy Ride

At the back section of our small farm was a field for planting crops. The area was remote from all roads and neighboring houses. To get to this area we had to travel back to a grassy lane between two other fields. It wasn't a long walk, but Kenny and I convinced Mother that we needed to take our 1958 Ford family automobile back to the field to haul drinking water and food, as well as having a place to rest from the sun. Daddy had earlier used the lane to teach us how to drive the car so Mother went along with the idea. Daddy was at work and Kenny and I were assigned to plow the field. We drove the tractor and car back to the field to begin our work. While we had the car in the open field we performed spin outs and spin arounds as the smoke roared from the tires. It was great fun and the folks never knew about our joy ride.
(Char's Note: You two are dreaming if you think they didn't know what you were up to).

158. The Neighborhood Girls

Occasionally we visited the Snyder girls who lived about a mile north on Hathaway Road. The younger kids of the family were Karen (Jerry's age) and Jean and June (twins that were my age). The remaining kids were Diane and Jim who were much older, and Bobbie who was younger. We did not become too close because they were girls with different interests than us boys.

159. Tractor Drag Racing

When we ran out of normal things to do on the farm, we would dream up some unique entertainment. One of these experiences was tractor drag racing. We took our old Massey Harris tractor down to the neighbor's house where our friend Danny Brewer lived and challenged him to a tractor drag race. Our Massey tractor beat their Oliver tractor "Hands Down" and we were very proud of our accomplishment. Afterwards we agreed to each other not to tell anybody because we knew if our dads found out, our butts would be dragging instead of the tractors.

160. Small Town Adventures

In Anita's entry you learned that Woodington, Ohio was a small town about three miles south west from our home. It was located on State Route 49 and the little town that provided a small church, a grain elevator, a barbershop, and a one room gas station. The town was put on the map by being the birth place of Lowell Thomas. The gas station owner had two gas pumps, and kept soft drinks and candy for sale. My brothers and I would ride our bikes to Terry Shiverdecker's house, which was on the way to Woodington, and hang out with the gas station owner named Isem Cox. He had chairs all around the inside of his little12 x 12 store and they allowed us to sit and talk with him about anything and everything. We would grab a large bottle of pop (12 cents); a candy bar (5 cents) and listen to Isem tell his tall stories. When he ran out of stories he seemed to make things up to keep the conversation going. I think Isem looked forward to our visits. Sometimes he would give us free pop just to keep us around.

161. Anita's First New Car

Before her first new car Anita bought a 1954 medium green used Chevrolet. I don't know where she bought the car or how old it was when she got it, but it was in very good condition. That was until she left the manual transmission in high gear at the top of the driveway and did not set the emergency brake. The incline and gravity of the driveway finally took over and we found her Chevy at the bottom of the driveway in front of the huge white concrete pillar with a major dent on the bumper and trunk. Daddy straightened it out the best he could and Anita learned a very important lesson in scientific gravity.

After high school she worked in several companies she saved enough money to buy a new car. Her new car was a 1960 Ford Falcon. It was medium tan and she was very excited to show it off. One summer day she noticed tar marks on the paint. She wanted to make the car shine and found it hard to remove the light tar lines with soap and water. She decided to use steel wool to remove the tar. Her method was working great until she noticed that the paint looked different everywhere the tar used to be. When she went to get Daddy, he found that every place she rubbed there was a loss of shine in the paint. Daddy used a buffing compound, and wax to restore the paint. He then told her that he would remove the tar the next time. The boys thought this was pretty funny and told Anita that anybody with brains would have known that steel wool is for scrubbing pans, not cars.

162. Anita's Boyfriends

Anita was very particular about the boys she dated. She required them to have the right amount of hair, the right hair color, the right color eyes, the right height, the right weight, the right personality and be of the right faith. In other words, the boy had to be perfect. Anita would bring a candidate in our house to meet the folks, and then she would ditch him after only one date if she found anything wrong. Most guys she dated did not stand a chance from the start. The boys tried to help Anita and participate in the critique exercise. We would generously offer our comments when Anita returned home from her date. Comments from the boys were, "He's a real loser, too short, bad car, bad hair, can't talk, too clumsy or we just don't like the clown. We were just trying to help weed out the duds from the possibility list. Something else we did to help out was that we made faces behind the losing candidates back. It was great fun.

163. The Blue Barn

Daddy had a thing about not wasting things and saving stuff. When it came time to paint our white barn, he bought the amount of white paint in 5 gallon cans that he felt was needed to get the job done. When he got to the last side of the barn, he saw he underestimated the paint supply and was running short. He found a gallon of very light blue paint from cans laying in storage and decided to mix this paint in the 5 gallon white bucket to stretch his paint supply. The mixture made the color a very pale blue tint and appeared to be only a little different color to the white already applied. Daddy knew this 5 gallon can of paint would cover the entire north side of the barn. He also figured that a person would only see one side of the barn at a time and did not feel the slight blue tint would be a problem. His decision was also based on the fact that he had already committed to the experiment and he was not about to throw away 5 gallons of paint. The paint was applied and when it dried, our dad was very surprised to find a beautiful powder blue barn. This side was also visible from the road when people approached our farm from the north. When we viewed the barn we knew our dad had created the only light blue barn in our community. I did have to admit that it was a beautiful color for a barn. Eventually he repainted the blue side back to pure white.

164. The Family Trip To California

In 1958 I was 11 years old. The folks decided to take the family on a train trip to California to visit Mother's brother, Francis Hittle and Dad's brother, Wayne Henkaline. They lived around the Los Angeles area. When the time came, we boarded the train at night in Greenville, Ohio. We found the train passenger cars were old, dimly lit, uncomfortable, ugly and noisy. I thought we had to go all the way to California on this car and I was concerned. Later we were told this was just the first part and when we got to Chicago the train ride would improve.

Upon arriving in Chicago, we ran into a small problem. Daddy found out that our tickets were not good until a week later. The ticket office finally agreed to let us continue but we had to ride in the last car of the train. It was great. The seats were plush; the whole side of the car was glass including the back and a wrap around glass roof. It took us a few days on the train to reach California. Mother packed us food to eat to avoid the high cost of the dining car and we slept in our seats. We could walk up and down the different cars and met some very nice people. As the train traveled west we could see the landscape begin to change from the flat land in the mid-west. I remember Daddy waking us up one morning to show us the western mountains. We opened our eyes, looked, said, "That's nice," and went back to sleep.

165. California – "Here We Come"

When we arrived in Los Angeles, it was nighttime. Uncle Wayne and Aunt Ann were waiting to take us to their home. We stayed with them and played with our cousins, Susan, Sandy, and Steve. We spent Christmas with them and they provided some great gifts for us. After Christmas, we traveled to visit Uncle Francis and Aunt Mary's home. We had a great time with our cousin Ann and they took us to Disneyland and Knott's Berry Farm.

Susan – Steve – Sandra At Uncle Wayne and Aunt Ann's' Home

Jack – Kenny – Jerry – Ann Hittle – and Steve Henkaline In California

Uncle Francis - Jack - Jerry - Mother - Anne - Kenny In California

Kenny And Jerry Became Strong Men In California

166. We're Going To Disneyland

Back in Ohio, we watched The Wonderful World of Disney on television, but we never thought we would ever find ourselves at the home of those famous characters. We saw Mickey Mouse, Minnie Mouse, Donald Duck and many other Disney Stars. We also saw many attractions and rode lots of rides for a full day of great fun.

The Henkaline Kids With Mother, Uncle Francis And Ann At Disneyland

At Knott's Berry Farm we saw western cowboys, visited an old saloon and saw gun fights on Main Street. We even panned for gold in a creek and took a sample of gold home as a souvenir.

Jack and Kenny Showing Their Stuff On A Bucking Horse
(Yes The Horse Was Stuffed Too)

167. My New Coronet

When I was in the 6th grade, it was announced by our teacher that if you were interested in playing a musical instrument you should raise your hand. I had not given this much thought until my best friend Mike Shade said, "Let's do it." I agreed and raised my hand. That night I asked my parents if I could play a musical instrument and they agreed to sign a paper for me to return to my teacher. This form requested a person from a local music store come to our house and speak with me and my parents about playing an instrument. The man showed up on Hathaway Road and explained about the variety of different instruments and how to purchase a new instrument. He brought several instruments for me to see and try out. Each was shiny and beautiful to see. Daddy wanted me to play the saxophone but I fell in love with the coronet. Mother and Dad finally gave in, and I had my very own coronet that night. It was the most wonderful thing that I was ever given and that I will never forget how proud I was to own that beautiful musical instrument. I think it cost around $125.00. That night, all I could do was make funny goose sounds from my coronet, and I did not want to put it down. What I did not know at that time was the wonderful musical experience I would gain and the love for music I was about to have from this decision.

The next week I was placed in the beginning band and was taught the basics of music and began to learn how to play my new coronet. Daddy took an interest in the instrument and we would go to the upstairs bathroom to practice every night. This room was selected because it was the most insulated place in the house to avoid the awful noise we made together. We would set the music on the back of the toilet tank and sit on chairs in front of the stool to try our hand at our new music adventure. I would play from the beginning music book then Dad would take his turn. As I became more proficient, I began leaving dad in the dust. He eventually found something else to do during my practice time. I think he did not want to slow me down. Even so, it was really great to have my Dad take an interest in what I liked to do.

168. A Snapshot Of Things In 1957

President Of The United States – Dwight D. Eisenhower
Vice President – Richard M. Nixon

Gallon Of Milk	$1.00
Loaf Of Bread	$.19
New Car	$2,100.00
Gallon Of Gas	$.24
New Home	$20,000.00
Average Income	$4,594.00
Dow Jones	435.69
Best Movie	The Bridge on the River Kwai – Directed by David Lean
Popular Songs	All Shook Up, performed by Elvis Presley Butterfly, performed by Andy Williams Don't Forbid Me, performed by Pat Boone Party Doll, performed by Buddy Knox Wake Up Little Susie, performed by The Everly Brothers You Send Me, performed by Sam Cooke Young Love, performed by Sonny James

169. Making Money Around The Farm

I began to work outside our farm when I was around 14 years old to earn money. Daddy helped Kenny and I get our first job. He knew a man named Len Sneery who lived nearby and was building a very large, new chicken house on his property. Daddy took Kenny and me to the site and convinced Mr. Sneery that we could be his gofers on the site and we would work cheap. Mr. Sneery agreed to give us a chance and we made $1.00 per hour for helping him. This led us into the chicken world, and we eventually did jobs like cleaning out the manure from the chicken house. To do this we placed the chicken waste on a mechanical manure spreader and took the spreader, pulled by a tractor, to the field.

Next, we helped transport the older laying chickens, who no longer would lay eggs, to the soup factory. We did this by reaching our hands into their laying cage and pulling them out by their legs. The chickens would try and peck our hands to keep from being caught so we had to use a quick grab technique to avoid this. After we got them out we placed them into a wooden crate which held about 10 chickens. The crates were stacked on a semi trailer for transportation to the butcher shop.

The final chicken job was de-beaking the chickens. The chicken house would be separated in half by a temporary wire fence after all the chickens were sent to one side. It was our job to round a small population of chickens up and put them in a smaller fence area and close them off. We would then grab each chicken by its legs and hand them over the halfway fence to a person standing on the other side of the fence. He was stationed at a machine to burn off half the chicken's beak. This did not hurt the chicken because the beak is like trimming our finger nails. He would de-beak the chicken to keep them from pecking others to death with their sharp beaks. This job paid us $1.00 per hour.

When we reached fifteen, we found jobs around area farms to bale hay and straw. There were several positions in the baling process which we did. One could be assigned to the wagon behind the baler and we took the bales of hay or straw from the baler being pulled from the tractor and stacked them six layers high on the wagon until full. Another job was to unload the wagon by placing the bales from the wagon onto a chain driven conveyor which took the bales to the barn storage loft. The final job was to be in the hay loft and stack the bales from the chain conveyor from the floor to the ceiling of the hay mow.

All these jobs were dirty, hot and very labor intensive. Each job mentioned paid only $1.00 per hour and we were glad to be able to make the money. The savings of our labor bought each Henkaline boy their first car and spending money for their Saturday nights. My first car cost $300.00 and I was able to pay cash for it and still have money left over to take Sharon on dates. The hard work set the stage for appreciation for a job and the work ethics we still have today.

170. The Boys Began To Farm

In the early days, farming the 56 acres on Hathaway Road was arranged with our neighbor Emmitt Welch. Daddy was paying off the bank loan and did not have the additional funds to buy all the equipment needed to plant and harvest the crops so he arranged a deal with Emmitt. They shared the cost of the grain to plant, Emmitt would provide the labor and equipment, plant the crop and they would split the profit 50% at the harvest. During these early years, Daddy also bought cattle, pigs and chickens to provide extra income and food for the table. The extra money he saved by farming provided funds for buying used equipment like a tractor, a wagon to haul hay, straw and grain, a two bottom plow, a disk for tilling, a drag for breaking up dirt clods, and a planter for seeding the grain into the soil. When we became teens, Daddy informed Emmitt that he and the boys were ready to take over our farm. When I was around fourteen years old, I remember getting off the school bus, changing into my work cloths and heading to the fields with the tractor and plow to prepare the ground for planting. Daddy and his boys worked as a team to make our little farm a successful investment for our family. Those were great times that I cannot thank my parents enough for the opportunity of learning to farm.

171. The Industrial Arts Project

I decided to take Industrial Arts Studies in my sophomore year of high school. One of the learning tools of this class was to teach us how to make wood projects. Our teacher was named Mr. Grabel, and he was a different type of teacher with little ability for having discipline in his class. I remember one time when one of his students (not me) decided to have a little fun and paint the door knob to our classroom with a shellac coating. The coating was invisible and when you grabbed the door knob you would quickly get the message what had happened. Mr. Grabel got the palm of his hand covered with shellac and became very angry at us. No one would own up to the trick and the bell rang to end the class and we all took off. Another personal interesting project that I encountered in his class was when I ordered the wood kit to make a large jewelry box. I attempted to sand the ends to make a good joint on the power sander. I just could not get the hang of fitting the joints to make a good fit. I would sand the end and could not get it straight. By the time I had my project completed I made a beautiful little cuff links box. The end joints were not very good and I think I received a "C" grade for that semester.

172. Jerry's Bologna Sandwich

After graduating from high school, Jerry worked in Union City, Indiana at Sheller Globe Hardy Division. Since he was drawing a paycheck, he gave the folks money for his room and meals. Mother would pack a lunch pail with a sandwich and some other types of good food. I don't recall where Mother and Daddy went, but Aunt Carrie agreed to stay at our house for a week and watch the boys. Kenny and I were still in school at the time. It was the first Monday night after work when Aunt Carrie quizzed Jerry about packing his lunch. Kenny and I were in the kitchen at the time when Jerry told Aunt Carrie how to make his sandwich. He said, "And I want my bologna sandwich this thick." He was holding his fingers over 1 inch apart. When he opened his lunch pail the next day, the bologna was over 1 inch thick between the two slices of bread. I think he fed his whole department that day. Jerry then had to explain to Aunt Carrie that he was just kidding. We determined that Aunt Carrie did not understand a good sense of humor.

173. My First And Second Car

I was 16 and had saved money to buy my first car. I found a 1956 Ford for $300.00 and made my first car purchase. The car had a six cylinder engine, was blue and white and looked good, but it had many mechanical problems. I had the opportunity to dump this junker when Jerry was ready to purchase his first new car. Dad convinced Jerry to trade my car in on his new car purchase and give me his 1956 Pontiac. This car was black with black interior. It had a big V-8 engine and was very fast. Jerry had already tested the speed of the car prior to my taking the title. I took posession and added special features like striping white tape to the metal dash, hanging white dice from the rearview mirror, adding blue running lights under the front bumper and putting small blue diamond buttons over the tail light lens. This car was used my entire high school time and provided great times and many miles.

Kenny and Jack In The Mid 60's

174. Free Gas

When I began driving a car, gasoline was at 25-cents per gallon. We never thought much about how cheap it was and how much it would cost to fill the gas tank. Dad had two 100 gallon gas tanks that he used to fill the tractor tanks. There was a bulk gas provider in Ansonia that drove their gas tanker trucks to the farm on a monthly basis to automatically fill the Henkaline tanks. The boys used this opportunity to fill their cars with gas from the tanks at no cost to them. Dad would quietly pay the bill and the boys would quietly take the gas. What a deal! This was another generous act my parents gave us that we took for granted.

Mother and Dad In The 1970's

175. My Dad

Dad was a hard working, God fearing, trustworthy man who was a great inspiration to the Henkaline kids. He worked as a final inspector at Hobart Manufacturing in Greenville, Ohio where Kitchen Aid mixers were manufactured. As a second job he managed the farm on Hathaway Road. Dad had polio as a young boy which caused problems with his feet. He wore high top work shoes with special insoles to adjust his arch for this condition. His feet would become very sore sometimes and he would soak them in hot salt water to relieve the pain. He never complained about his feet deficiencies and would go about his chores with energy and enthusiasm. Dad would rise up every weekday morning at 4:00 am to feed and bed down the livestock and then head to work. When he arrived home around 4:00 pm we immediately ate dinner so he could attend to the additional farm chores. He would milk the cows, feed the animals and maintain daily chores before dark. During the spring and summer months he would plow and disk the fields, plant the crops and make necessary repairs to the equipment and buildings. Also he planted and tended to a large garden so we could have canned vegetables during the winter months. We all called him Daddy when we were young and I changed his name to Dad in my mid teens. He taught his kids by example. Honesty and integrity were never in question when it came to our parents. They were well respected by all who knew them in our community.

Dad's favorite Song was *How Great Thou Art*. I looked up the song for this book and discovered why my Dad liked it so well. The words you see below highlight how awesome our God is, that He created the universe with his hands, and all that is within it. The song goes on to tell how Christ will come back to earth someday and take His believers back with Him to heaven. It finally describes the joy we will have to bow before him in adoration and proclaim how great Thou art".

How Great Thou Art
Lyrics ~ Carl Boberg, 1859 - 1940
English Translation ~ Stuart K. Hine, 1899 -

Stanza 1:
O Lord my God,
When I in awesome wonder
Consider all
The works Thy Hand hath made,
I see the stars,
I hear the mighty thunder,
Thy pow'r throughout
The universe displayed;

Stanza 2:
When through the woods
And forest glades I wander
I hear the birds
Sing sweetly in the trees;
When I look down
From lofty mountain grandeur
And hear the brook
And feel the gentle breeze;

Stanza 3:
When Christ shall come,
With shouts of acclamation,
And take me home,
What joy shall fill my heart!
Then I shall bow
In humble adoration
And there proclaim,
"My God, how great Thou art!"

Refrain:
Then sings my soul,
My Saviour God, to Thee,
How great Thou art!
How great Thou art!
Then sings my soul,
My Saviour God, to Thee,
How great Thou art!
How great Thou art!

Dad would drop words of wisdom in timely situations as he was around us. I recall the following statements as an example of his teachings. When we were working on a project like making something or painting he would say: "Now stand back and see how it looks before you finish." When he was paying a bill he would say, "Pay on time and if you can't, "Go to the other person and tell them how you are going to pay them." Other comments like, "Always be honest," "Don't lie," "Don't be afraid to tell the truth," and "Do it right the first time," were just a few of the teachings we learned from our Dad. They still stick in my mind today some 50 years later. *He was a Great Dad!*

176. My Mother

Mother was a hard working homemaker. She was always there when any of her kids needed something. I can look back and see that my Mother was one of the most generous people I have ever known. She would quietly sacrifice and not expect anything in return. She helped with the livestock chores as well as keeping the house clean and the kids in line. She was an excellent cook and provided a meat and potatoes dinner almost every day. I remember her reading her Bible frequently on our back enclosed porch. She taught Sunday School at our church and studied her lesson every Saturday night. She did not have a high school education but she was a very smart lady. She would show us God through her quiet ways and gently nudge us a little closer to Him by her statements and daily activities. She worked very hard to teach every one of us addition, subtraction, multiplication and division. Sometimes it was hard to learn our school lessons and we ended up telling her that we couldn't understand it, with crying and many tears. Our mother would not let up until she knew that we understood the lesson. There were no home school lesson plans she could purchase when she tutored each kid. Mother would teach and probe us about Jesus and our salvation. I know she was an important part of my religious beliefs today and I will always be grateful to her. I look forward to thanking her again when I see her in heaven. To sum it up, my Mother was **'The Best'**. I love her greatly and appreciate her more than I can ever say. I owe her a lot for a great deal of my basic knowledge skills and her spiritual wisdom. Many of my good traits came from the teaching of my mother. I thank God for giving me this wonderful person I call 'My Mother'.

177. My Sister Anita

Jerry – Kenny – Anita – Jack

Anita was a person who I always admired as a big sister and a person to look up to. Since she was nine years older than me, we obviously grew up in a different space age. Even with the age gap, I remember her protecting me and my brothers and giving her special love to her younger siblings. I can't remember having a fight with her as I grew up. She always seemed to be helpful around the Henkaline house and I know my parents were very proud of her. As she grew up to be a young lady, I was always proud to say, "That's my sister."

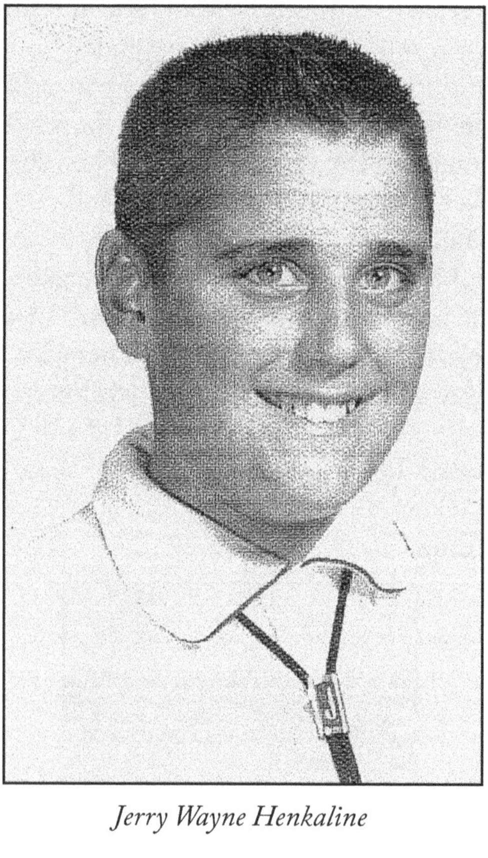

Jerry Wayne Henkaline

178. My Older Brother Jerry

Jerry loved any type of sports and he was good at any sporting event he participated in. In our early childhood years, he usually didn't want me around but he knew he had to tolerate me because I had no plans to leave the family. I remember the time when he was 16 years old, had his drivers' license and wanted to borrow the family car for a Saturday night in Greenville. Jerry had a few school buddies named Charlie Baughman, Marvin Peters and Terry Pepple. They had plans to cruise the streets of Greenville, Ohio and check out the chicks. I somehow convinced my Dad into telling Jerry that I should go with him if he wanted to borrow the family car. Jerry strongly argued his case stating that I would not be welcomed by his friends, but Dad stood his ground and I got to go along. It was a pretty uneventful evening and I really felt out of place. Although Jerry didn't want me along, he didn't give me a hard time and treated me with respect among his friends. After that night, I respected his privacy and never asked to go again.

As we got older, Jerry and I became even closer. I will never forget the time when I was in the Army taking my advance training in Fort Belvoir, Virginia. Sharon and I were newly married and she had secured a civil service position at the military post and came to live with me in an apartment. It was our first Christmas together and we were very sad to be away from our family. To make things worse I had just wrecked our 1965 Mustang when I crashed into the back of another serviceman's car on post. I did not see him stop to turn left and the collision put our car out of commission. We did not have transportation and no way to get home. Jerry was working at Sheller-Globe in Union City and contacted me to inform me that he would pay the round trip bus fare for a trip back to Ohio to enjoy Christmas with the family. We jumped at the chance and had a great Christmas. We boarded a Greyhound bus late one afternoon in Alexanderia, Virginia and arrived in Dayton, Ohio the next morning. I will never forget how generous my big brother was to us. I was really touched that he cared enough for Sharon and me to be home for Christmas.

Kenneth Gene Henkaline

179. My Younger Brother Ken

Kenny and I seemed to be closer growing up. We formed the club house and slept out on Friday nights with our cousin Terry Shiverdecker. We roamed the country side in the bright moonlight, baked home made pizza for the late night snack and topped the evening off by looking at adult magazines. We rode our bikes together to Woodington to meet Terry at the Isem Cox's small store for a Coke and a candy bar. We would sit inside his crowded store and exchange true and fictional stories. Isem would love to see us come. Not only did he make some sales of his goods, but he loved to get involved in the conversation. I remember several winter evenings when I went ice skating on a remote pond near Woodington, Ohio with Kenny and Terry. It was great fun and exciting to find a remote pond away from population. Kenny has the ability to take things apart and remember how to put them back together. I admired him for his mechanical talents. I had some great times with my little brother in our growing up years.

180. The Sister I Did Not Know

Joyce Ann Henkaline was born October 24, 1943 and lived only one month and one day with a sickness called whooping cough. I often wonder what she would have been like as a sister. When I watch the Jimmy Stewart and Donna Reed movie, "It's A Wonderful Life, the story makes me think about Joyce and wonder how she would have influenced my life and the lives of the Henkaline kids. We would have had great fun with her and I think Anita would have loved to have had a sister to share and defend against the brothers. I can't help but believe that she would have grown up to be a successful person and become a fine representation of the Henkaline family. I can't wait to see her in heaven and share my love for her. I expect her to run up to me and say "Hi, I'm your Sister, Joyce. Let me show you around Heaven.

181. A New Trumpet

I graduated through the elementary Ansonia Band Program and entered the Junior High Band. I really took an interest in music and became very good at playing my coronet. Mother and Dad saw my musical talent flourishing and decided to buy me a new trumpet. I think my dad had a vision for me to become a great trumpet player in a professional band or go to college to become a band director. Dad announced one day that he was willing to buy me a new trumpet to encourage my interest in music. Soon I went from playing the coronet to a wonderful Con Constellation Trumpet. This trumpet was the top of its class and it cost my parents over $300.00 at the time. Nobody that I knew had a trumpet this grand and I still play it today. I later graduated to the high school band and after a couple years was placed in first trumpet section and later was awarded the first chair of first trumpet. This was the top position in trumpet section.

182. Entering My Mid Teens

I was a freshman in High School in 1963 and I began to realize there were pretty girls out there. I wanted to explore my feelings about why I was beginning to become attracted to them. I was placed in our high school band beside a very pretty blond girl named Sharon Brown. I knew who she was, but I didn't give her much attention.

At the time, I had a heavy crush on a high school senior named Carol Shade. Carol was an older sister to my best friend Mike. She was very nice to me and she knew that I really liked her. She was dating another guy in her class and she knew this thing with me would go nowhere. One day Carol told me that she knew a girl who really liked me. I was curious so I asked her who this girl might be. She told me "Sharon Brown really likes you." Carol went on to say, "I mean, she really likes you!" This got my curiosity going and I made it a point to talk to Sharon at the first opportunity. We got to be good friends and the more I was around Sharon the more I enjoyed her company. I looked forward to band practice time and the chance to sit beside her in the trumpet section.

Soon I forgot about Carol and wanted to spend all my time with Sharon. She was the prettiest girl in the band as well as her class. I did not know why she liked me, but I certainly was not going to ask. One Saturday morning, later that year, we were at a band rehearsal practice and were taking our instruments and music from the band room to the gym across the hall. I didn't see Sharon coming out of the band room door and she didn't see me going in. We met suddenly at the doorway and she kissed me for the first time. This was my very first kiss from a girl and I almost couldn't contain my excitement. At that time cupid struck me with both arrows and I knew that this was the girl I wanted to fall in love with.

We dated later that year and before we graduated from high school we began making plans for our wedding and future. She is still the love of my life and my best friend. I am grateful for what Sharon saw in me and the music events that brought us together. As I look back on the chain of events, it all makes clear sense to me. In elementary school a guy named Mike Shade convinced me to raise my hand when our teacher asked who might be interested in playing a musical instrument. He later decided to change his mind and never played a musical instrument. I chose a cornet over a saxophone when the man came to our home to show us instruments. Sharon also chose a trumpet as her choice of musical instruments. We both entered school with a different path not knowing each other. We ended up setting beside each other in the trumpet section. Carol Shade, sister of Mike convinced me to talk to Sharon. The interest and love of music brought Sharon and me together. And finally God's plan for music in our lives began to develop through His pathway that He put in place long before we were born.

183. Challenging For Chairs

It didn't take me long to learn that a girl named Sharon Brown, who also played a trumpet, wanted the top spot in the trumpet section of the band. I held the first trumpet position and she announced that she wanted to challenge me for the position. The procedure to gain a higher chair required the challenger, and the challenged person, to audition before the band director. The director selected the music and heard both musicians play their part. He then assigned the best person to the higher position. Sharon won the first audition and I lost my position as the top section player. When we were allowed to challenge again, I made the challenge to her and won my spot back. We switched the role a couple of times throughout the year until Sharon graduated from high school and left me "King of the Hill." I think we both were pretty good trumpet players, but I honestly knew Sharon was the best musician between us. As seniors, Sharon and I each won "The John Philip Susa Award" in our respective years. This award was presented to the best musician in the entire band and given to a member of the Senior Class

Jack – Junior Year Picture

184. Love Letters From Sharon

During our high school days, Sharon and I would see each other as much as possible at school. I would make it a point to see her, if only for a minute, between classes. Sometimes we would pass a love letter along and head for our next class. Just seeing Sharon come down the hall towards me with her beautiful smile would make my heart jump a quick beat. If she gave me a letter, I would make it my first priority to read after I sat down at my next class. Her hand writing was beautiful and anything she wrote was music to my ears. The words, "I love you" and "I miss you" made me want to be with her even more.

Jack and Sharon At The Ansonia Senior Prom

185. Our Dating Nights

I couldn't spend enough time with Sharon during our dating days. I would drive to Rossburg on Friday night and we would go cruising the entire night in downtown Greenville and sometimes we would go to a movie. On Saturday night you might see us at the Greenville drive in to watch a double feature. Sharon loved to eat one of the shredded barbeque sandwiches at the food concession at intermission and I loved to please Sharon so I bought her as many as she wanted. We also dated on Sunday night I would sometimes take her with me to the Missionary Alliance Church when I played in a trumpet quartet. I did not care where we went as long as I was with her.

There were a couple special eating places we visited when we went to Greenville during our dates. One was called Frisch's Big Boy Restaurant. You could drive in, park your car and go inside to eat. Most of the time everybody backed their car into a parking spot and the restaurant provided curb service. While we waited for our food we watched scores of cars pass by that were cruising the streets of Greenville. The cruising course took you from the Greenville downtown area out to Frisch's (which was about two miles out of town) then back to downtown. This route was a continuous stream of teenager cars during the weekend.

Another place we went to grab a sandwich to eat as we cruised was called The Maid-Rite Drive In. This unique little spot provided a special ground beef sandwich in a bun with a special secret recipe that everyone wanted. There were always many cars lined up at this fast food restaurant to buy their sandwiches, chips and drink. There wasn't a good place to park at the Maid-Rite after you purchased your food so we usually just ate as we cruised downtown. A great feature at the Maid-Rite was the wall between the drive up windows. The first window opening was where the person took our order and money. At the next window was where we received our white sack with the sandwiches, chips and drink. Between the windows was where you placed your chewing gum on the wall. It became a work of art on where and how you placed your used gum.

The Maid-Rite Drive-In

Customers Place Chewing Gum On The Wall While Waiting For Their Order

186. Asking Sharon To Marry Me

Sharon and I went steady, which meant we were committed to each other, and dated in our final years of high school. It was in my senior year that I asked her to marry me, and she said yes. Many of my friends did not know how I landed the most beautiful girl in our school. I didn't either but was not about to ask her why she chose me to be her future husband. Sharon was not only beautiful, but smart. She had a great personality and was very popular in the entire school. She won a local talent and beauty contest in Versailles, Ohio around her freshman year of school. In her senior year she participated in the Harvest Queen Contest in Arcanum, Ohio. It was a beauty and talent contest that included girls from every school in the county. Sharon won the contest and was crowned Arcanum Harvest Queen.

LAW OFFICES
ENGELKEN & COX
ATTORNEYS AT LAW

JOHN E. ENGELKEN
CORNER FOURTH & WALNUT
GREENVILLE, OHIO 45331
TELEPHONE 548-1920
AREA CODE 513

HERBERT W. COX
ARCANUM NATIONAL BANK BLDG.
ARCANUM, OHIO 45304
TELEPHONE 692-8320
AREA CODE 513

October 23, 1964

Sharon Brown
323 Ross St.
Ansonia, Ohio

Your Majesty:

I want to personally thank you for participating in the Arcanum Harvest Queen Contest.

All the young ladies were so lovely that the judges' choice was made difficult in the extreme.

If you are a representative of tomorrow's generation, I'm sure our country will continue to be the world's leader on all fronts.

With warmest regards and best wishes, I am

Very truly yours,

Herbert W. Cox
Queen Contest Chairman

HWC:mj

Sharon – Senior Year Picture

As the grand finale, Sharon was elected the Ansonia Senior Homecoming Queen. She could have had as many guys as she wanted falling all over her to date, but I was the lucky one she chose. Sharon was a year ahead of me in school and graduated in 1965. After graduating she found a job in civil service working at Wright Patterson Air Force Base in Fairborn, Ohio. We decided that after I graduated, and found a job, we would get married. We selected the date of August 12, 1966 for our wedding date. I felt like the luckiest guy in the world that day and thanked God for such a wonderful girl to marry. For our wedding, we had to select a church. I was a member of the Christian and Missionary Alliance church in Greenville, Ohio and Sharon was a member of the Methodist Church in Rossburg, Ohio. Since my church had just built a new large sanctuary and Sharon's church was fairly small, we decided to get married in the larger church. Sharon and her mother worked out all the details of the wedding with some help from my mother. Sharon's mother made her wedding dress by hand and it was breath taking. When I saw Sharon for the first time in that dress coming down the aisle to meet me I almost could not stand the excitement and joy that entered my heart. I kept thinking, "This beautiful girl has agreed to marry me." Family members were selected to be part of the official ceremony and that hot day in mid August became perfect.

187. Our Wedding Day – August 12, 1966

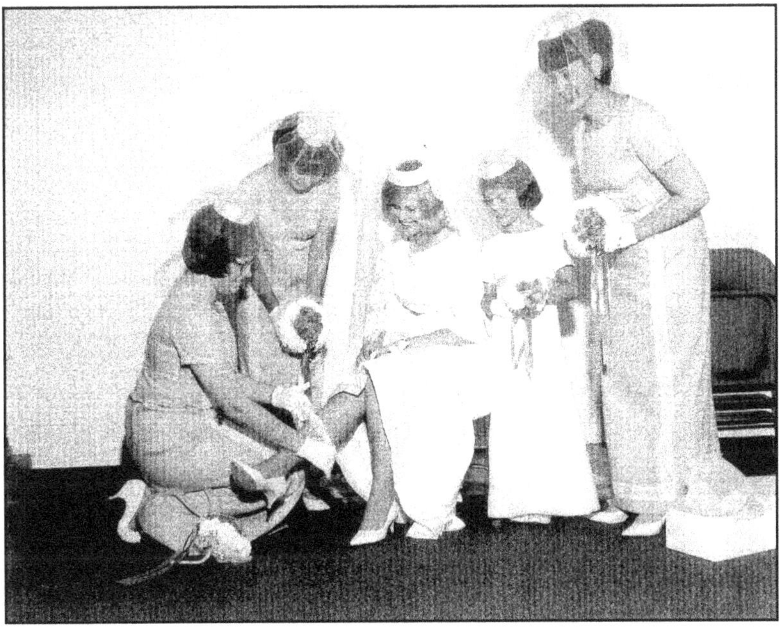

Pam Bell, Darla Brown, Sharon, Elaine Harter and Anita Henkaline placing the garter in place before the wedding

Sharon And Her Dad Coming Up The Aisle To Greet Her New Husband

The New Married Couple

Parents Of The Wedding Couple
Left - Ron and Pauline Brown - Middle - Sharon and Jack
Right - Olive and Bill Henkaline

Far Rear
Reverend Fred Isch -
Back Row
Anita Henkaline – Darla Brown – Pam Bell – Sharon and Jack Henkaline – Jerry Henkaline – Ken Henkaline – Mike Shade
Front Row
Elaine Harter (Flower Girl) and Brother Billy Harter (Ring Bearer) – Both Cousins of Sharon

188. My First Real Job

Before graduating from high school, I had landed my first job to begin my career. The job search for me was pretty easy because of Mother and Dad and the neighbors across the road on Hathaway. Neighbors Emmitt and Irene Welch, had a relative who was in a key management position within a food distributor company located in West Carrollton, Ohio. West Carrollton is located approximately 10 miles south of

Dayton, Ohio. The manager set up an interview for me at White Villa prior to graduation and I landed the job. I think my neighbors had the job secured for me before I arrived for my interview. Another factor that I learned was that my new job was a "go-fer" position and the salary was at the bottom of the pay scale, so awarding the job to me was a plus for both me and White Villa. Another important fact was that Sharon had secured a job as a legal secretary at Wright Patterson Air Force Base near Dayton. The job offer was perfect. I found a single bedroom, with a shared the bath in West Carrolton, which was owned and occupied by an elderly lady. Sharon had a room at the Dayton YWCA. This meant that we could meet every evening prior to our wedding date.

White Villa was a warehouse company that stocked large quantities of food and then distributed on to small grocery stores within a 100 mile radius on a weekly basis. My first day at White Villa was to meet the management and my new boss Earl Faulk. He was a kind, middle aged man with a cigar in his mouth at all times. He quickly explained how he took the grocery store orders from a large computer spread sheet and planned the daily semi-truck deliveries to various grocery store routes in Ohio, Indiana and Kentucky. The key was to plan the truck route schedule in proper order as efficiently as possible and place the food order in the semi-trailer so the last grocery store delivery was first in the trailer and the first delivery order was placed last in the trailer. This little task took some job knowledge, such as which truck route was assigned to the correct state and area, where the store was located on the route, what their order for the week consisted of and would all the orders assigned to the truck route fit in the trailer. Earl had worked in his position for many years and had a mental visual picture of all these details and how to match the order with the route. Another little factor that needed to be considered was that the food order consisted of cans, boxed food, as well as cool refrigerated items and frozen foods. The semi-trailers were not refrigerated so this meant the cooler/freezer portion of the order had to be place at the end of each order so the un-loader could get them off the truck quickly and into the grocery store cooler/freezer as soon as possible on a hot day. If this sounds complicated......it was. I attempted to understand the truck route map by trying to memorize each route and the stores within the route. The total population was multi-store locations in each route and which came first to last on the route. Earl was not the most efficient trainer and trained me "on the fly." It did not take him long to understand that I was best used as his go-fer boy. One day he had more tasks than he could handle so he gave me one truck route to schedule. I completed the task and held my breath to hear that everything went well on my scheduled route. The next day Earl informed me that he had a very upset semi driver, because I had scheduled the load by packing the first stop at the nose of the trailer. In other words, the entire trailer load had to be removed at the first stop to get their order located in the nose of the trailer. From then on it was "Hey Jack, I need you to go out and check for this inventory item, or "Hey Jack," I need you to stay here and answer the phone for me." Even this did not work out too well because when I answered the phone the caller would not want to speak to anyone except Earl. We did not have cell phones, pagers or walkie talkies available back then so I had to walk out and try to find Earl. When I returned to the phone to tell them Earl was on the way, the caller had lost patience and hung up. This did not please Earl that he had a frustrated caller, but he had great patients (or sympathy) for me. Earl's problem was finally solved when I got my letter in the mail from Uncle Sam to tell me the United States Army had different future plans for me. Earl was very understanding of my short stay, but I noticed that he did not say, "You be sure and come back to us after you've finish your Army assignment."

189. Our 1965 Mustang Convertible

I can join the hundreds of thousands of people who have said, "I sure wish I still had that car." Before we were married, Sharon and I both wanted to buy a Ford Mustang convertible. We admired them on the new car lots but just couldn't feel we were able to afford one. We were driving in the Dayton metropolitan area one day and spotted it. I can still remember seeing that car on the lot and even remember the name of the used car dealer, Dick Rue Motor Sales. Our find was a black 1965 Ford Mustang convertible with a black top. The interior was also black, and it even came with a cover to be placed over the interior when the top was down. The tail lights were modified with red lenses and chrome bars that covered most of the rear of the car. It had beautiful magnesium rims and even sported an air conditioner, which was rare in those years in a vehicle. We stopped to look at it and decided we had to have it. After some financing paperwork was completed, we drove that pretty little car off the lot and into our lives. We paid $2,100.00 for it and couldn't have been happier with our new set of wheels. Our ownership was short because we felt we had to sell it when I entered the Army and got orders to travel overseas. We eventually sold it for less than what we paid for it, but the great times we had in that beautiful car were worth every penny.

190. Uncle Sam Say's, 'I WANT YOU'!

After our wedding on August 12, 1966, Sharon and I had settled in an apartment in Oakwood, Ohio. I was at White Villa in West Carrolton, Ohio (near Dayton) and Sharon was employed in Fairborn, Ohio as a legal secretary at Wright Patterson Air Force Base. We rented the upstairs apartment as our first home together. Things were going great for us for about three weeks. Then Sharon went to the mail box one day after returning home from work and found a letter from Uncle Sam. It read, "Dear Jack, your friends and neighbors want you to report to your local draft board and serve in the U.S. Army." Sharon was in tears when I got home as she handed me the letter. We both went into shock and did not know what to do or think. Our short married life was about to be turned upside-down and there was nothing we could do about it.

191. Reporting For Duty In The U.S. Army

I reported to my draft board in September of 1966 in Greenville, Ohio. I was sworn in that day and transported to Fort Knox for my basic training. Basic training is where the Army accelerates the civilian into the military basic functions in record time. We left Greenville on a Greyhound bus and arrived at Fort Knox around 11:00 pm. The next day we were assigned into a twenty man platoon and met our Drill Sergeant who I will never forget. His name was Sergeant Austin. He was a short, well built man with a southern accent. He immediately let us know that he was our new boss and taught us that when he gave the order to jump, we only had to figure how high. We received our military clothing and Sergeant Austin led us to a very old wooden two story building with an open bay on each floor that we would call home for the next two months. I was assigned to a bunk and was taught how to make a bed military style. In the next eight weeks I received plenty of vaccinations, learned how to march military style, how to shoot a rifle and how to insert a bayonet on the end of my rifle to kill people. We got plenty of physical exercise by running up and down hills and doing push ups and jumping jacks.

Sharon visited me every other weekend while I was in Basic Training. She remained at her job at Wright Patterson during my basic training. My next assignment was advanced training at Fort Belvoir, Virginia. This fort is located approximately 25 miles from Washington D.C. Sharon transferred her civil service government job from Wright Patterson to a government job in the U.S. Army personnel office in Fort Belvoir. After receiving her new job assignment she and her mother traveled to the area to find an apartment for us. They drove our 1965 Ford Mustang convertible with as many personal items as it would hold. Living quarters were hard to find, but Sharon and her mother found a small two bedroom unit at Woodbridge Apartments in Woodbridge, Virginia. The rent was high, but it seemed to be the only thing available, and we knew we would only be there a few months. Woodbridge was approximately 12 miles from the post and Sharon could drop me off at my training site before she went to work. Once settled we took Sharon's mother to Washington DC to return to Ohio by bus. It was a very happy day to have my new wife living with me again. We rented the basic furniture, which included a television, and only bought what we needed for our short stay.

Sharon began her new job in the Army personnel office and worked for Army Staff Sergeant Travis. He was responsible for handling assignments of Army personnel from the post to their permanent duty station when advanced training was complete. My training assignment was called Missile Equipment Repair and consisted of the repair equipment in a Nike missile underground site. We learned to fix anything that might go wrong with equipment that would cause a malfunction during lift-off in a world crisis. I was about to complete my training and learned my upcoming permanent orders would take me to South Korea. This was an assignment that the wives could not join the husband. When Sharon learned the news she went to work the next day crying. When Sergeant Travis saw her crying he asked what was wrong. She explained about permanent assignment and that she could not go with me. He liked Sharon and her work, so he calmed her down and told her not to worry too much about my orders. In a couple of days, he told her that my orders had been changed and I was assigned to stay at Fort Belvoir as an instructor to train others in missile equipment repair. His real intentions were to keep Sharon working for him.

She was elated and couldn't wait to tell me the news when she picked me up to go home that night. She explained that since her Sergeant was the one who cut the orders he could also change the orders. We both were grateful with the news and thought our next two years in Virginia would be great. This good news only lasted for about one week. It was then when Sergeant Travis called Sharon to his office and explained that another lady working in his area learned about my shift in orders and complained to him about it. The lady explained that her son had just received orders to Viet Nam and what was happening with me was not right. Sergeant Travis explained that to keep this lady quiet, and keep him out of trouble, he would need to change my orders to an overseas assignment. He went on to say that Berlin, Germany was the best assignment possible at the time and I had been cut orders to go there. He assured Sharon that she could join me to Berlin. He also said that I would be given a two week leave prior to heading to Berlin. Finally he explained there was one other little requirement to make this happen, and to keep him out of trouble with his commander. I would have to go to the Pentagon in Washington D.C. to meet a Colonel to sign the final assignment. Sharon got the date and directions from Sergeant Travis and explained the news to me that night.

I drove our car to Washington D.C. and located the Pentagon. I found a parking area near the entry. If you can imagine, there are top brass from all branches of the military assigned to the Pentagon and I was at the lowest rank of enlisted personnel. As I began to walk towards the Pentagon, I found myself saluting so much my hand was in a continuous up and down motion the entire walk. I think I even began saluting park benches and lamp posts during my travel, thinking they might out rank me. After many inquiries inside the enormous Pentagon building, I finally reported in to the office where I was to meet my full bird Colonel for his approval to seal my permanent duty orders. I waited for about 45 minutes in an outer office and a lady finally came up to me and said the Colonel had to attend a very important meeting and would not be meeting me. She said that he instructed me to return back to my post at Fort Belvoir. I was a little confused but followed her directions. Sharon explained my experience to Sergeant Travis and he said not to worry about a thing because everything was covered.

My training was completed two weeks later and our unit was making the final plans to go to Korea. Each day during the last week, Sergeant Travis assured Sharon that my orders were finalized and for me to just keep my mouth shut and wait for them to arrive at my Unit Commanders office. I obeyed his directions. The day before we were to ship out for Korea I had heard nothing of my special orders to Berlin. I went home that night and told Sharon that since I had heard nothing of the changed orders, I had to pack my duffel bag for the assignment to Korea. We both were very scared and didn't sleep much that night. We began to wonder if something else had gone wrong with Sergeant Travis' plan. Sharon dropped me off at my assigned barracks and I waited in fear that I would not see her again for one year. I was frantic and told my Sergeant that I just learned that I had been given different orders and asked if he could check this out. He just laughed at me and told me to go back and join the others in my unit. We were instructed to pile our duffel bags in a place where they would be picked up later that morning. We had nothing else to do but wait so our Sergeant instructed us to go outside and pick up cigarette butts off the ground. When we returned I was called into his office to face a 'Not so happy Sergeant'. In his angered voice, he said "I don't know who you know or how you did this, but you have been re-assigned to Germany and you also have a fourteen day pass." He then said, Get you're sorry tail and your stuff and get out of my sight." I was so excited that all I could say was, "Yes Sergeant" and scrambled to a phone to call Sharon about the great news. She thanked Sergeant Travis and picked me up to make plans to pack our things and drive back to Ohio to be with our family. It was a great time-off before

I left for Germany. Sharon stayed home for a short time until I was able to call for her to come to Berlin.

Sharon And Jack On Military Leave In Rossburg, Ohio

192. My Permanent Army Assignment

I was assigned to the 40th Armor Tank Division in Berlin, Germany. The Post was made up of approximately 32 tanks and support units. The purpose of the 40th Armor tank company was to show presence and power to the East German government. Our tank exterior surfaces were sanded, cleaned and painted at least semi annually. The paint on the tank was a high gloss that looked like a shiny new car. The mechanics in our unit kept them running in tip top shape. Since I had no training on a tank or in mechanics, I was assigned to the maintenance office as a clerk. I eventually was given a ¾ ton civilian pick-up truck to make part runs from our post to other military supply part areas in Berlin. This was a great job!

Company "F" 40th Armor Tank In Parade – "See How It Shines"

193. Sharon Arrives In Berlin

After a little over a month in Berlin, I sent for Sharon. It was a Saturday morning and I was eagerly waiting for my new wife to join me. The city of Berlin had a population of 2.2 million people and featured two large metropolitan airports. Sharon arrived at one Berlin airport and I was waiting for her at the other. When I learned of my error I was frantic. I ran to a taxi and yelled at the driver to take me to the other airport "Snell" (German for Fast). I could see my beautiful wife standing in fear in a strange foreign airport where she knew no German, and wondering where I was. To say the least, I was a basket case. I arrived at the airport and ran to her gate. We finally met, fell in each others arms and were happy to be together. I took her to a little German house that had an upstairs rented as an apartment. That year, we began an exciting adventure as a young couple. We were very much in love and wide-eyed to see the world outside of Ohio.

Jack In His Army Fatigue Work Clothes

Jack and Sharon While In Berlin, Germany

194. Our Little German Apartment House

I learned about the German apartment from a GI in my company who was transferring back home at the same time Sharon was coming. I looked at the place and felt it was suitable for us to survive until something better came along. The owner of the house was a wonderful German man. His home had a section missing where it was bombed during WW 2. It appeared to us that he was in no hurry to rebuild his house. He lived in the lower lever with his mother and rented the top floor to service men. We accessed our apartment through a closed stairway which led to an upstairs landing. At the top of the landing we could enter our apartment which consisted of a large furnished living room and a bedroom. The upstairs landing also led to a bathroom and a kitchen that we shared with the owners. That was the extent of our living quarters. It was small but we didn't care as long as we were together. We learned after moving in the house that it was located about 1 mile from the Berlin Wall.

Our landlord was a very nice man. One evening he invited us to his living room for coffee and cookies. He spoke only German and we spoke only English. A little vocal and a lot of sign language were used during our visit. He began to show us pictures from his past. We learned that during the war he was a prisoner. His past did not affect our relationship and later we privately titled him as "The Prisoner." One day when I arrived home from my post, The Prisoner was working on his little German car in front of his house. I was in my work fatigues and he asked me to hop in for a ride. Sharon didn't know that I was home and I thought we were just going around the block. What happened after we began our drive began to concern me. He drove his car to the end of the street and directly towards the Berlin Wall. We drove up to a high fenced area in the outskirts of the city. Between the two fences there was barbed wire with land mines to stop anybody from the east down who wanted to cross into the west. There were many high tower structures along the fence which housed guards with weapons, spot lights and guard dogs. Our journey ended up within 25 feet from the fenced area. My landlord stopped his car, got out and began talking to a German Solider on guard duty. I just stood by the car wondering if

I was going to be taken hostage or was being used as an American token. He finally returned to the car, jabbered some German and we drove back to the apartment. That visit was as close as I wanted to be around two Germans when I did not know the plan.

Fence Separating West Berlin From East Berlin
Fence – Middle Barrier With Mines - High Fence With Barbed Wire

195. The Visit To East Berlin

While stationed in Berlin, US service men were issued a special pass to cross the wall and into East Berlin. The official purpose was for us to sightsee but the real reason was to allow us to shop the stores and pick up some great buys. We were given a one day pass and we were required to wear our military dress uniform. I think our government wanted the East German people to see the presence of US service men stationed in West Berlin. A couple of days before we left for our visit to the East, I went to a West Berlin bank and purchased East German money. The exchange rate from the dollar to East German money was twenty-five cents to one dollar. Then, we took this money exchange to East Berlin and were able to get even a greater bargain on our purchases.

On one of my East German visits I drove my 1961 Volkswagen through the American Checkpoint, then the Russian Checkpoint and finally through the East Checkpoint. We were required to get out at Checkpoint Charley (US checkpoint) but only stop and show our pass through the windshield at the Russian and East German gates. Once we were in East Berlin, we were allowed to travel freely but were advised to stay within given areas of the city to stay out of trouble and so that we could find our way back to the west. I always took an army buddy with me on my visits. We also had good directions where to shop from previous GI visits and planned to visit the high shopping points. I wanted to purchase a wooden ship that was a model of the Mayflower, and we were given directions to the store. We found that it was a tobacco and pipe store which had the model ship I wanted. After entering the store, I told the man behind the counter that I wanted to purchase the ship. He spoke perfect English and said he would place the ship in a box for me. I was surprised to hear him speak English and I told him that I was also looking for a grandmother wall clock. He quietly said, "I know what you mean, but we will have to wait until the couple in the store buying tobacco leave." My buddy and I stood there puzzled but followed his direction. As soon as the couple left, the owner locked the front door and walked back behind his counter. He pulled open a floor trap door and asked us to follow him into a basement. I hesitated but thought there are two of us and one of him so we followed him down the steps to a small basement. He walked to a shelf and pulled out a very ornate wooden grandmother clock. It was very beautiful and beyond my expectations. I asked him the price and he told me in East German currency. The cost in dollars was $18.00. I could not believe my find. He told us that he would get the winding key and have the clock wrapped for us to pick up in one hour. We returned and the clock was purchased. Later we learned the tobacco store was a government run establishment and the man was selling his goods on the side. When we returned on my next East Berlin visit, the store was vacant. My guess is that he sold some of his private inventory to the wrong East German people.

Jack Standing In Front Of Brandenburg Gate In East Berlin

196. Announcement Of Our Child

A couple of months after arriving in Berlin we learned that Sharon was pregnant with our first child. We were very excited and arranged a call back to Ohio to break the news to both our parents at the same time. I think they were also pretty excited and made us promise to keep them updated throughout Sharon's pregnancy. Our son, Christopher Blaine Henkaline, was born May 21, 1968. We had purchased a 1961 used Volkswagen and Sharon obtained her driving permit to drive in Berlin. I was sent to a field exercise the day that Sharon drove herself to the US Army hospital for a routine last check up. During her examination the doctor told her that she was in labor and needed to be admitted immediately to have her baby. I was called in from the field when Sharon was about to deliver. Her labor time from the examination to the delivery time was 1 ½ hours. A couple of days later we took our son home to begin our little family.

Our Little Boy On His First Day Home From The Hospital

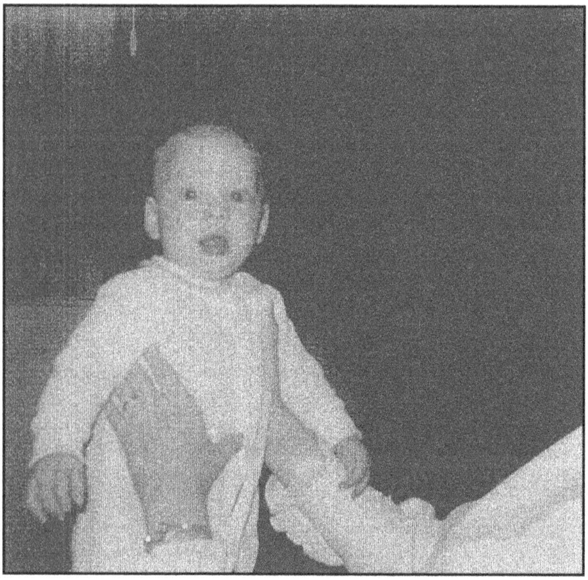

Chris - Standing Up In Berlin

197. Apartment Moves Around Berlin

We moved to five apartments in the city during our stay in Berlin. It wasn't hard to move because most everything we had consisted of a small dinner place setting, a few pots and pans, some bedding sheets and blankets, our clothes, shaving gear and cosmetics and a small black and white television. A few trips in our VW beetle was our moving van.

From The Prisoner's house, we moved to a 5-story high rise apartment building called "The Sweet Beat." The name was given to the building because the entire street level section was a German Teen Age Nightclub. The second floor housed administrative offices and floors 3 through 5 were apartments The building developer designed heavy insulation between each floor, but the sound of the music and bass vibration could still be heard from the giant speakers on lower levels. Every weekend the place would be packed and rock with teenagers coming in to drink and dance to German and American Music. If your apartment was unfortunate enough to be located on the 3rd floor, you would be put to sleep by the thump – thump – thump of the low bass sound. Sweet Beat apartments were hard to rent and most were quickly taken by military service personnel because they were modern, convenient and low rent. The apartment set up was very small and as basic as you could imagine. It consisted of an entrance hallway, a built in kitchen in the hallway with a small under-counter refrigerator and small counter top range. The bath had room for one person and consisted of a sink, toilet and a shower/tub combination. The short entrance hallway led to one open room. A small furnished round table provided a place to eat. A compact bed folded out from the wall. The room was our dining, living, closet and bedroom combined. Even our closet was built into the wall. We jumped at the chance to get in and tolerated the noise because we really liked the modern apartment, military friends in the building and the value for rent. The noise from the night club finally became too much and we moved to another older German apartment. Within six months we returned back to the Sweet Beat to be with our old friends, but this time we found an apartment on the 4th floor. The last year of our stay in Berlin we became seasoned American residents to the German economy. We chose a few close friends and spent our free time on the weekends with them.

Our final residence was a small German house in the city approximately 10 miles from my 40th Armor Post. We found this place from another military friend in my company who we met in our first stay in The Sweet Beat. They had lived in the little house and were returning to the United States. There was bus transportation near this little German house and we had our reliable 1961 VW Beetle so the distance to the post was not a problem.

The owners of the house were Herr and Frau Teeitz. They were both in their late 60's, retired and wonderful German people who became our overseas grandparents. Their home was a cottage type home in a quiet little German neighborhood. It had a cobblestone sidewalk and a picket fence in the front. On the sides and back of the house was a beautiful yard with well trimmed trees, beautiful flowers and a small fruit and vegetable garden. They rented the back portion of their home to us, which consisted of a small kitchen, a large living and dining combination room with an adjoining bedroom that had an open arch and a small bathroom. We fell in love with the house, the private setting and our new landlords.

We learned from our new landlords that a couple of favors from us would make our stay more pleasant. Herr Teeitz smoked a pipe and he asked me to purchase American tobacco from our post exchange. He felt our tobacco was a better quality and our Post Exchange price was half the cost of German stores. Frau Teeitz asked Sharon to buy a 5 pound bag of sugar for her each month. They paid for the purchase and we were glad to pick up their requests when we went grocery shopping at the Post Exchange.

There was one inconvenience that we had to overcome in our new little German apartment. Getting hot water to take a shower was an event and not a reaction. To obtain hot water for our shower we were required to put charcoal briquettes in a small chamber under a 15 gallon tank reservoir. The tank was solid copper and was located in the bathroom. This chore took about 15 minutes to get the briquettes burning and one hour to heat the water. Sharon and my showers were back to back events and we were not allowed to take long showers. The hot water for hand and dish washing was provided by a 2 gallon hot water heater above each sink. We turned the heater knob on and it took about 30 minutes to get hot water. The heater was on a timer and the water in the little heater would finally cool and require you to turn it on again for the next use.

One early evening we were surprised by an explosion in our kitchen. Sharon was preparing for our evening meal when smoke came pouring out of the oven. I looked at the situation and immediately went running for Herr Teeitz. It didn't take him long to find the problem. He opened the oven door, looked in, and smiled pointing toward Chris. Then he showed us two flashlight batteries in the back of the oven that our young son previously put in. The heat of our oven expanded and exploded the batteries. Herr and Frau Teeitz loved us and really loved our little boy. They frequently took him by the hand to their back yard to pick and eat strawberries. Our stay with Herr and Frau Teeitz was our best and we were grateful to have the opportunity to spend time with them.

198. Sharon Meets A Vision In The Night

We were still at Herr and Frau Teeitz apartment when Chris became very sick. He was about 6-months old and had a high fever so we took him to the US Army emergency hospital for an examination. The doctor said that he had a bad cold and sent us home with medication and told us to give him a cool bath. We did as directed and put him down for the night. We retired early and I was sound asleep. Approximately 3:00 am Sharon was startled from her sleep and sat straight up in bed. She opened her eyes and saw a dark gray figure standing at the foot of our bed. The room was pitch dark and the figure could be seen in the dark. It had no face, no eyes and wore a dark gray cloak with a hood. She rubbed her eyes but the form did not go away. It then moved from the foot of our bed to Chris's crib and bent over looking down at him. Sharon immediately got up and the form immediately disappeared from sight. She went to the crib and picked Chris up to check on him. What she found was one of his small blankets was wrapped around his neck and was beginning to strangle him. Sharon held our baby the rest of the night in her arms and thanked God for sparing his life. I have never heard of one of God's angels appearing in dark gray and I wonder if it could have been a demon angle coming from Satan. What I do know is that God's power woke Sharon and protected Chris from death. We are both confident that our God spared our child that night and that He had some very important work for Chris to accomplish in his life on earth.

199. Vacation Visits Around Europe

After Chris was a bounding healthy baby we decided to explore Europe. Sharon's parents decided to make a trip to Berlin to see us and their new grandson. During their stay we showed them the Berlin sites and then planned a trip to Western Germany. I made arrangements for us to take the military duty train out of Berlin to Frankfort. After arriving, I rented a car and we began our trip to see Garmisch Germany, the Bavarian Alps and the beautiful German castles in the mountain country side. While driving, I received a speeding ticket from a German police and had to pay a fine on the spot for my crime. We saw the most beautiful castles with gold appointed interior walls and furniture. Sharon and I had a great time with her parents and we cherish those memories with them.

Grandpa Ron Holding Chris

Sharon and I took another trip to Western Germany to Italy and Switzerland. We took a train from Frankfurt into the cities of Augsburg, Germany - Rome, Italy - Pisa, Italy – Milan, Italy - Venice, Italy and Innsbruck, Austria. Since our baby had a head of bright blond hair, he was a hit with all the dark haired Italian people. While in Rome we stayed at a hotel near the Vatican. We met some Catholic Sisters from a church in Cleveland, Ohio and had a good conversation with them. When you are this far away from home, anybody from your home state is just like the next door neighbor. One of the Sisters asked if we had seen the Vatican and we said we would be going in the next couple of days. She said, "Would you like to see the Pope?" We said, "Sure that would be great." We weren't Catholic, but we knew this would be an honor. She explained that her parish was going to see the Pope the next day and we could join them. She said there would be tickets in our hotel mail box the next morning and we should use them to go in. The next morning I went to the front desk and told the clerk that we had some tickets in our room mail box to see the Pope. He said, "I am sure you do." To his amazement, he returned with two blue tickets in hand. We inquired how this would work and he explained that we would not be able to take our baby with us during the visit. We listened carefully and thanked him for his explanation. We both knew that we would not leave our baby alone with anybody, no matter who we would get to see. We did visit the main sites of the Vatican that day with Christopher but not in the presence of the Pope. We still have the tickets today in a picture frame.

200. Sharon Heads Home

Sharon left Frankfurt, Germany on August 16, 1969. We purchased a one way ticket for her and Christopher on TWA airlines and the ticket cost only $150.00. Because of stormy weather conditions. her flight continued to circle New York City and when she finally landed, her plane to Dayton had already departed. The family was gathered at the Dayton airport and got word from TWA that Sharon would not be coming in until the next morning. They returned the next day to greet Sharon and meet Christopher.

Mother And Dad Meets Their New Grandson For The First Time

201. I Came Home Next

I was given an honorable discharge from the Army on August 25, 1969. It was a very happy day to arrive back in the United States and begin my civilian life again. I retuned to my old job at White Villa and we moved to an apartment in West Carrolton, Ohio. The job had not changed from previously working there prior to my draft notice so this stay only lasted for about 6 months. I quit and took a temporary job in the area until I could find a more suitable position. We wanted to be closer to our families so I found a job in Union City, Indiana at the Sheller-Globe Hardy Plant. We settled in Greenville, Ohio which is approximately 15 miles from Union City. I accepted the job and our life seemed to be back on track again.

I began as a job time keeper, and eventually was offered a position as a laboratory technician. This position allowed me to begin my career in Quality. I eventually worked my way through the Sheller- Globe organization. I was transferred to the Sheller-Globe Grabill plant and became the Quality Manager. I was later promoted to the Corporate Office in the Education Department and held the position of Manager of Employee Involvement and Plant Training Manager for all plant locations. In the Employee Involvement arena I received a national award from the Association for Quality and Participation which was given to the best individual in the United States representing Employee Involvement. During my time at the corporate level I managed 30 plant locations in Employee Involvement Teams. Our company was awarded the best Team Award in the nation for two consecutive years. Sheller-Globe was very good to me and opened many doors to excel in my career, improve my skills and broaden my abilities. I traveled across the United States, Canada, Mexico and Great Britain to train plant associates new techniques in the area of quality and participation. I believe the core reason for my successful career was based on basic training that came from Dad. He taught his children to work hard at what you do, offer the best effort you can, and over deliver in everything you do.

202. A Strangers Kindness Never Forgotten

The year was 1970 when I got a job working at Sheller-Globe in Union City, Indiana. I needed transportation from Greenville to Union City and we owned only one car. It was a used 1967 Volkswagen Beetle and served our transportation needs well until we needed a second car to get Sharon to work in Greenville and me to work in Union City. I shared a ride with another worker for awhile and asked around at work about other cars for sale. I learned from a friend that he owned a big red Oldsmobile with plenty of miles but in fairly good shape. We looked at the car; it fit our budget of $200.00, so we bought it and named it Lester. Since I worked 2nd shift, I arrived at work at 3:00 pm and left for home at 11:30 pm. I learned of a short cut on a back road about five miles from work to the main route into Greenville. Lester ran great until one night he stopped running dead in his tracks. I knew he had plenty of gas but Lester showed no signs of life. I got out of the car and began to walk to the nearest house for help. Keep in mind, at this time, there were no BlackBerry's, I Phone's or even a cell phone invented. This type of personal communication was not even in our wildest dreams. The time was around 12:00 midnight and I felt lucky there was a home just down the road with a light showing through the window. I knocked on the back door and a man came to answer. I told him, my car had stopped and it had plenty of gas so I would need to take it to a mechanic the next day. I explained that I worked 2nd shift and I had just left work and was going home. He said to wait on the porch and quietly went back into his home. A couple of minutes later he returned with car keys and said that he wanted me to take his car to my home and I could bring it back in the morning after I got some sleep. I was taken back by his generosity and realized this was my best option. He had a nice clean car that was much better than any I had ever owned. I retuned his car with a full tank of gas the next morning after having Lester towed to a garage in Union City. I offered to pay for the use of his car but he insisted that would not be necessary. It struck me that morning, how much faith and trust this man had in me. He didn't know me, didn't know my name other than who I said I was, but he trusted me with his valuable possession to return it the next day. This man's kindness and faith has never left me, and I have applied his kind actions several times to others. Each time I offer a kind act to somebody in need, I tell them, "I don't need thanks or money, but rather for you to offer somebody else the same favor you just received from me." I do not know my guardian angel's name, but because of his kindness to me, I have passed it on to others.

203. A Call For Help

At the time, I was working at the Sheller-Globe Grabill, Indiana plant as the Quality Manager. Some of the perks of this position was that I had a private office and was able to use the company telephone watts line to make free long distance calls in the United States whenever I chose. Since we had moved from Greenville to Van Wert, Ohio, I made regular calls to find out what was the latest news from home. One day on my lunch period I decided to make a call to my parents. The phone began to ring and no one answered within several rings so I placed the telephone call on speaker phone and listened to it ring while I worked on some paperwork. The phone continuously rang and I continued to work. The length of time eventually became ridiculous and for some reason I decided to make this a little game to see how many times I could let the phone ring before the system cut me off. After a long period and to my surprise a woman's voice answered on the other end. This voice did not sound like my mother. I grabbed my hand set and said "Who is this?" The voice said, "This is Mother and I need help right now". I quickly asked what was wrong and she said that she had passed out on the living room floor and could barely breathe. She continued to explain that she had crawled to the telephone and that Dad was sitting in the front yard and she did not have the strength to reach him. She quickly stated again that she could not breathe and needed somebody to help her. I told her to hang up her telephone and I would call 911 for an ambulance. I then hung up my telephone receiver and immediately called my Indiana operator to help me get through to the Greenville emergency number. Once the call was made and help was on the way, I tried to contact one of their neighbors to enter their house and help my mother get her breath. My attempts failed so I had to sit at my desk helplessly wondering if the emergency rescue would get to my mother in time.

What I learned later that day was that my Dad was sitting on his lawn chair in their driveway enjoying the day. He said that he heard the sirens from a distance coming his way. He then saw them turn on Knoll Avenue and pull into his driveway. He asked what they wanted and they explained that somebody in his house called for help and they needed to go inside immediately. He was shocked to hear this but led them to his front door and they found mother sitting on the floor gasping for her breath. She was given oxygen and transported to the Greenville Hospital. We learned later that she experienced a severe bronchitis attack and the lack of oxygen caused her to pass out. Mother soon recovered and things got back to normal. I thanked God that he directed me to choose to call that day and allowed me to play my telephone ringing game so I could get Mother the help she needed.

Our 1967 Volkswagen With Bozo

204. Our 1967 Volkswagen

Uncle Jerry and Aunt Char bought an air inflated Bozo Clown for Chris to use as a punching bag and one day he ended up in our 1967 Volkswagen. He was a bad driver. The Volkswagen was a good car and we had a lot of fun with it.

205. Looking Back On My Life

Reflections.....It is now the year 2013. As I reflect back over 47 years, I remember the day I saw Sharon coming down the church aisle. She was the most beautiful girl that I have ever seen. Not only beautiful with outside appearance, but she also was smart and acquired a kind heart and a wonderful spirit. I knew at that time how lucky I was that she chose me to be her soul mate for life. Back then we shared a beginning love that bonded us together.

Soon after our wedding day our lives took a sudden turn in the road with a letter from Uncle Sam. We were shocked and devastated when I received that draft notice only one month after our wedding day. When I look back on this, it is clear that God took us away from our families at this time for a purpose. I feel that it was in His plan to mature us as a young married couple by isolating us in a foreign country. We had to depend on each other to form our initial bond in marriage. I believe our love has matured and blossomed because of this experience early in life. Over the years we have grown closer because we know each others heart and soul and we share common dreams to share our happiness. We learn and laugh together and have peaceful moments side by side.

Yes, I love to remember the yesterdays but the most important times are the today's and our forever's. I owe a lot to Sharon for many reasons. During high school we dated as soon as I obtained my driver license. This may not seem like an important event but I sometimes wonder if I would have gotten into trouble with the high school friends during my young days exploring with those wild oats. Later when I served my country and was sent to a foreign country, I was very lucky to have my beautiful young bride with me. I am confident that she kept me out of trouble when I saw fellow soldiers around me drinking in bars and searching for German girls to seek romance.

Sharon and I have experienced many wonderful times, some difficult and some times that only a deep love for each other could get us through the trial. Today we don't navigate like we once did and have lost our youthful appearance, but I can honestly say that I love Sharon more now than the day I married her. I know our love was meant to be and I believe our first kiss was as much a part of God's plan as the stars in the night sky. God had His hand in bringing us together and I couldn't have chosen a better person to share my life. I believe that the life we share reflects His love, day by day. I thank God for Sharon with all my soul and love her with all my heart.

CHAPTER 5

Kenneth Gene Henkaline

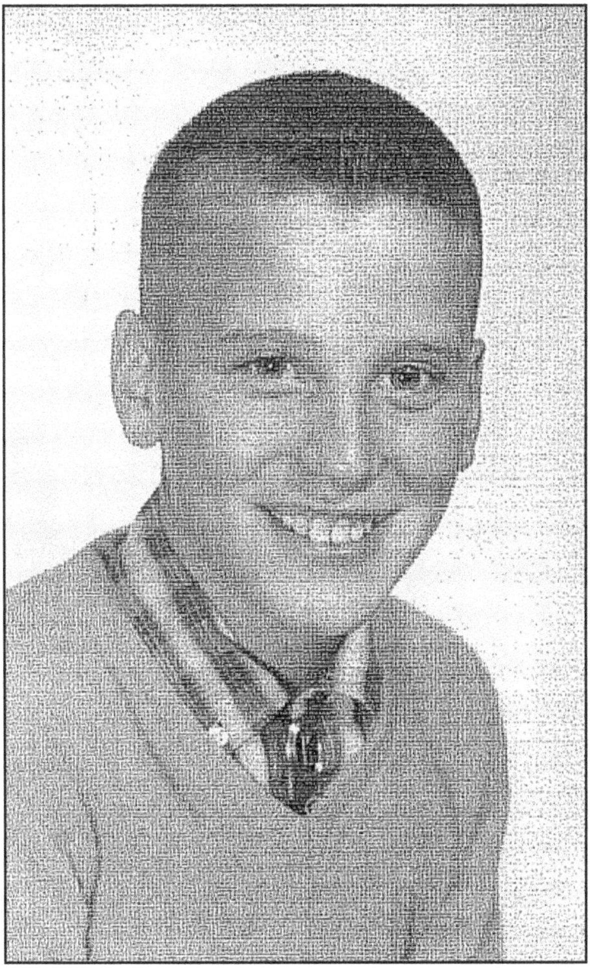

206. Ken - The Haymow Hideouts.

When the haymow was full of hay it was time to build the hideouts. The tunnels were easy to build. All it took was two rows of hay bales set apart by about 2 feet and then cap them with hay bales across the top. If you wanted a higher tunnel, just stack the rows on each side higher. The main room at the end of the tunnel was a little more tricky. You had to cover the top by finding long wood supports to span the width and length of the area. The span could not be too wide or the ceiling would collapse by the weight of the hay on top or by somebody walking over the area. I tried to outdo myself with one of my hideout designs. The tunnel went in two directions and led to a very spacious main room in the middle of the haymow. The main tunnel led along the outside barn walls so the light outside entered through the cracks of the siding. My only problem was no light in the main room. No problem, I thought. I just went to the house and found matches and candles. I lit the candles at the beginning of the tunnel and transported them to the main room. What I didn't think about was the combustible hay all around me. Fortunately for me, no fire was started. Now I know why Mother and Dad's hair turned gray so quickly.

Kenny With Sled In Front Yard

207. Halloween Prank

When I was in high school, I remember a Halloween time when fifteen classmates and I decided to go pranking. We fit all sixteen in Bobby Dynes station wagon. We drove north on St. Rt. 118 until we found a farm that had corn stalks. The stalks were brought together and tied in a bundle to dry. We decided it would be fun to knock over the corn stalks.

It was a cool night with a full moon and plenty of illumination to see our work. We parked the car one field away from the crime scene. We walked to the field to do the dirty deed. As we were having our fun knocking over the corn shalks, we heard a dog barking in the distance. The sound of barking became closer and closer. We thought that it might be the farmer and his dog had discovered that we were trespassing on his property. We calmly began to cross the field and head back to our car. All of a sudden, we heard gun shots and the bullets were hitting all around us. Mike Doyle, our football center, was just ahead of me on the run. I can remember Mike putting his hands on the fence and hurdling it without touching. It was amazing how fast you can run and jump when somebody is spitting lead at you. I was one of the last ones to reach the car and the others had already started to make their exit. The back door of the station wagon was open and someone grabbed me to pull me in.

As we were driving back to Ansonia, scared out of our wits, we went around a curve too fast and the weight of 16 people broke the car axle. We were stranded. Our plan was to keep 14 people with the stranded car and two to walk back to Ansonia to get Bobby Dyne's dad's tow truck. Rick Bickle and Bobby drew the short straws to walk back. During their walk they became tired and decided to hitchhike a ride back to town. To their amazement, who would stop to give them a ride, but the farmer! He inquired as to why they needed a ride and they made up a story of their country walk. It all seemed to work out until he noticed one of his corn stalks on the back of Rick's sweatshirt. He did not give them a ride back to town but rather a ride back to the 14 waiting trespassers. We begged mercy and promised to set the corn back the next day. To do this we had to skip the first half of school the next day. When we went to school at noon the principal was waiting for us and knew of the corn stalk prank. To our surprise there was no disciplinary action. Don't you love it when a plan comes together?

208. Favorite Memories Of Dad

As a little boy, one of my favorite memories of my Dad was the one-on-one time we spent together. We would head back to what we referred to as the back forty, which was basically a field and wooded area, to go exploring. As we walked back the grassy lane, with a fence on both sides to separate two fields, Dad would put me on his shoulders and I would feel like I was on top of the world. We would walk through the woods exploring trees, wild flowers, insects and the beauty of the woods and solitude. I felt the love that my dad had for me. My dad was as loving, gentle and honest man as I have ever known. I feel that he passed on to me his human compassion to me and all the Henkaline family.

209. Memories About My Mother

My mother gave unselfishly to all her family without expectations of return. She gave us much love, cleaned our clothes, cleaned the house, and taught us right from wrong. I remember times when she taught us school work assignments at the kitchen table. What I did not know at the time was that her formal education only went to the 8th grade. She would open the school book and we would learn together. She also taught us character and honesty. She was a gentle, loving, Godly person. I feel blessed by God to have her as my mother.

210. Hot times In The Henkaline House

I remember the nights during the hot days of summer. It was so hot, that I couldn't sleep, so I found a cool spot under the pear tree in the front yard of our house. I would gather up my sheets and pillow, call our dog, Lassie, and spread the sheets out under the tree. I would spend the rest of the night in the cool and solitude of the country air. Sometimes I would enjoy the beauty of a full moon. When I woke up the next morning, I could feel the cool dampness of the morning dew. Those great memories will be with me forever. Maybe that is why I enjoy the great outdoors today.

211. Why I Should Have Been An Engineer

When I was a boy, I was always inquisitive about how things worked. I would disassemble almost anything just to see how and why it worked. I had a moped that I tore completely apart and laid all the disassembled parts on the garage floor. They were arranged in the sequence of how they were disassembled. I would clean and inspect each part before I put the assembly back together. Also, I painted the frame with a gold paint. Sometimes I would have to engineer a new part to replace the one that was worn out. I remember Pop coming out, looking at the sprawled out parts, shaking his head and saying, "You will never be able to get that mess back together again." I proved him wrong and the final product looked better and ran better than before.

212. My New Schwinn Bicycle

After receiving my new bicycle for Christmas, I was curious how the back brakes worked when you reversed the pedal. So I thought the only thing to do was to tear it apart and see how it worked. I found out that the brakes worked with a series of different sized and shaped washers. I dropped the washers as I was disassembling the bike, and lost the sequence for reassembly. It took me the biggest part of the day, by trial and error, to figure out how to correctly reassemble the brakes to make them work again. But, I did learn how and why coaster brakes work. Maybe that's why my goal in life is to build a working Robot.

213. The Sticky Fingers

When I was very young, Grandma Henkaline would visit our home often. She was an Avon Sales Representative and carried a black leather bag with all the products. She brought the bag to our home on one occasion. When Grandma wasn't looking my curiosity got the best of me and I opened the bag to see what was inside. Among other things, I found a comb in a plastic jacket. I felt that I needed it more than she did, so I took it. After thinking about it, my conscience began to haunt me that I stole something that was not mine. Rather than doing the right thing and admitting my guilt, I thought "out of site, out of mind." I went to the barn, got a shovel and buried the comb behind the corn shed. At the time nobody ever knew, but I know now it was the wrong thing to do.

214. Mothers Funeral

When Mother passed away we were all devastated. Pops had died just eight months earlier. Mother had just returned from the Holy Land and was rushed to the hospital with a heart attack. At the funeral home we had a family visitation prior to opening up to public viewing. She looked very beautiful and peaceful in her casket. As the boys were viewing the casket, Wally wanted to take a picture of her. We all discussed if this would be appropriate. It was finally agreed that since this was a private viewing it would be okay to take the picture. Brother Jerry then said, "Let's take it as a family portrait." We all thought this was a great idea. Since Mother was in the prone position, this became a problem. We knew the casket wasn't big enough for all of us to get in, so Jerry suggested that we sit Mother up on the edge of the casket. (At this point I must make a disclaimer that the boys have a warped sense of humor and like to play practical jokes on others.) Now to accomplish this task, we knew her hips and legs would need to be broken so she would look beautiful in the picture. It was now time to gather the girls to share our plan. When we gathered them around the casket, Brother Jerry explained our plan. Anita just about had a cow and said, "No Way!" The funeral director accidently overheard the conversation and walked away shaking his head. We thought Mother would be laughing along with us in this practical joke we played on Anita. We did this prank with the greatest respect to our loving mother.

Anita's Note: This still isn't funny, even though Mother, no doubt would have laughed about it all.

Jack – Kenny – Jerry At Mother's Funeral

215. Miserable Visits From Uncle Bud

As a hair stylist, one concern should be focusing on the clients that are in your chair. That was hard to do when Uncle Bud would decide to visit me, walk right in, pull up a chair beside me and start talking about the same old stories about the ground hogs digging holes in the foundation of his barn, having to buy new tractor tires, slopping his hogs, going to buy his winter coat at Farm and Fleet and other stories that I have heard a thousand times before. I, or my clients, had no interest in his conversation whatsoever. After awhile, I would say, "Uncle Bud, I have an appointment with my banker and I have to run. " I was such a liar, but I have to do what I have to do.

Ken With His Pontiac GTO At Knoll Avenue In Greenville, Ohio

216. My First Heartbreak

When I was a sophomore in high school, I met my first love at the Christian Missionary Alliance Church. Her name was Julie Brown. We dated about 3 ½ years. She attended Greenville High School and I attended Ansonia High School. After high school she attended Cedar Point College and I worked at New Idea in Coldwater, Ohio. When she would come home on the weekends, we would date. These dates became more infrequent as time went on. She would say she would have to study and could not see me. What I did not realize at this time was that she wasn't studying but rather dating another guy. One weekend when I knew she was home, I called to ask her out for a movie and dinner. Her mother answered the phone and said, "We need to talk." I met her mother at their home and she said to sit down because I have something to tell you that is not pleasant. She went on to say that Julie had been dating somebody else and she just moved to California to be with him. I was devastated. At the time, this was the saddest time of my life. Two weeks later I saw their wedding announced in the local newspaper. What I did not know at the time, was that God had a special plan to give me a wonderful girl named Julie Fess to be my wife and a darling daughter named Lindsay to become another one of my children. Julie and Lindsay became the perfect addition to my other beautiful children Heather and Heath. I truly believe that they all are a special gift from God to complete my life.

CHAPTER 6

Later Homes And Final Days

217. Homes And Life After Hathaway Road

On January 5, 1944, Mother and Dad bought the farm on Hathaway Road from George W. Miller for $7,501.00. They lived there for 24 years until Daddy's full retirement. It was then that they realized the farm upkeep was more than they could handle so they made the decision to sell the farm and move to Greenville to purchase a home. On August 18, 1968 the farm was sold to Paul Knick for $39,000.00. They purchased a nice, well-built home in Greenville on Knoll Avenue. This home provided a large living /dining room combination, an eat-in kitchen, one bath and two bedrooms. It had a one car garage and nicely landscaped large back yard consisting of fruit trees, raspberry bushes and an area to grow a vegetable garden. The property also had many trees for the grandchildren to climb. They lived in this home until 1974 when Dad's health began to rapidly decline.

100 Knoll Avenue – Greenville, Ohio (Picture Taken 2011)

Their next move was to a small efficiency apartment in Greenville located on Main Street. This apartment was very small and was built next to a creek that ran through town. To avoid water overflow into the building area the developer built a retaining wall between the creek and the parking area in front of the apartments. The only view that could be seen from the front windows was blacktop, the retaining wall and the creek. Soon after moving my dad announced how much he hated this place and he called their home, "The Pit." He made it very vocal that he wanted to move to a new place that had more room and a nice view. Mother tried to encourage Dad by stating how efficient there apartment was with inexpensive rent. She felt that time would get him accustomed to it. She soon realized that he was not going to change his mind.

The Entrance Door To "The Pit" Apartment (Picture Taken 2011)

The Front Window View From "The Pit" (Picture Taken 2011)

Anita came home for a visit and had a little chat with Dad on how things were going. He explained to her how dissatisfied he was with their apartment. During her stay Anita decided to look at several nice places for rent to lift Dad's spirits. She and Mother found a very attractive apartment located on the north side of Greenville on Chippewa Street. The price was reasonable and she and Mother agreed that Dad's last days should have nice memories and should be a place that he liked. Anita described the apartment she had seen to Dad saying that it had a nice front and back yard, had a garage and was located on a quiet street not far from where they lived. She went on to say the interior was spacious, well kept and it had many windows to make it bright and cheery. It took no convincing to tell the landlord they would take the place. They signed the lease and Dad loved it. He stayed there until poor health finally took him to the Greenville Hospital on August 11, 1983

The Apartment On Chippewa Street (Picture Taken 2011)

218. Dad's Death

Mother took great care of Dad during his illness and in his final year at home. He had a disease called sclerodermas which attacked and hardened his vital organs. He was admitted into the Greenville Hospital on August 11, 1983. His stay lasted 14 days until his death on August 25, 1983. His spirits were high in his final days and we never heard one complaint during our visits. When he could no longer talk, he would look at us with his beautiful blue eyes and smile. We told him how much we loved him before his final breath.

219. Mother's Time After Dad Died

Anita convinced Mother to return to Colorado Springs, Colorado with her family after Dad's funeral and when things were settled down. Mother retuned home to Greenville and was adjusting to her single life. In May 1984, Anita and Wally convinced her to take a trip to the Holy Land. We encouraged her to make the trip and told her this was once in a lifetime opportunity. She was very excited and decided to go. Upon her return she had lots of great stories to tell and brought back some very nice gifts for us.

220. Mother's Death

Approximately two weeks after returning from her Holy Land trip, Mother was admitted to the Hospital in Greenville with a severe heart attack. Her doctor informed us that her heart had extreme damage and if another attack occurred it most likely would be fatal. The boys rushed to her side and called Anita to return home as soon as possible. We spoke to Mother while in intensive care and her spirits were high. Anita was rushing back from Colorado Springs and Jerry and Jack left the hospital to pick her up in Dayton. When we returned to the hospital and arrived at the hallway to the intensive care room Ken met us and informed us that she had another acute heart attack and was gone. We were taken to a small chapel in the hospital to deal with the shock and collect ourselves. Looking back on the quickness of Mother's death we were grateful that she did not suffer and was now with Dad in Heaven.

The Final Resting Place
Ansonia Cemetery
Ansonia, Ohio

CHAPTER 7

The Grandchildren

Beverly – Ken – Chris   Back Row
Keith – Heather – Missie – Ty – Travis   Middle Row
Heath – Lindsay – Trent   Front Row

This photo was taken the day of their Grandmother Henkaline's funeral. It was the only day that all the cousins were together at one time.

Left to Right – Ken – Wally – Keith – Beverly - Anita

Back Row – Missie – Jerry – Ty - Char

Front Row Trent - Travis

Sharon – Chris - Jack

Back Row Julie – Ken – Lindsay

Front Row – Heather – Heath

CHAPTER 8

A Special Memorial To Missie Henkaline Kogge

In Loving Memory of

Melissa "Missie" Kogge

1971 - 2007

221. Missie Henkaline Kogge

Missie was Jerry' and Char's oldest child, and was born October 16, 1971. Missie married Marc Kogge on April 22, 1995 and they had four children. Wesley, Taylor, Andrew and Katie, Twins. Our beloved Missie was taken from us by a tragic automobile accident on January 17, 2007, at 35 years old.

222. A Passage Read In Honor Of Missie

Canon Henry Scott-Holland, 1847-1918, Canon of St Paul's Cathedral
Death is nothing at all
I have only slipped away into the next room
I am I and you are you
Whatever we were to each other
That we are still
Call me by my old familiar name
Speak to me in the easy way you always used
Put no difference into your tone
Wear no forced air of solemnity or sorrow
Laugh as we always laughed
At the little jokes we always enjoyed together
Play, smile, think of me, and pray for me
Let my name be ever the household word that it always was
Let it be spoken without effort
Without the ghost of a shadow in it
Life means all that it ever meant
It is the same as it ever was
There is absolute unbroken continuity
What is death but a negligible accident?
Why should I be out of mind?
Because I am out of sight?
I am waiting for you for an interval
Somewhere very near
Just around the corner
All is well.
Nothing is past; nothing is lost
One brief moment and all will be as it was before
How we shall laugh at the trouble of parting when we meet again!

223. Missie's Story

From little on, Missie liked to talk and to be on the go. She took her first step the day she was eight and a half months old and never stopped moving after that day. Her first word was actually a sentence, "Where's the puppy?" and once that was spoken she never stopped talking. When Travis was little he did not talk and actually was taken to doctors twice because there was worry that he may not be able to speak. Travis and Char walked Missie to pre-school on her first day and when they walked back into the house Travis asked for a drink of water. Char was stunned and said, "Travis, you talked." His response, "I can always talk." Apparently, up to that point, speech was not necessary because Missie did all the talking for both of them.

224. Swimming

Being on the go meant being social and Missie wanted to be doing, learning and joining. She wanted to be in the water and learn to swim when she was three and the local pool would not take anyone that young for lessons. When Missie was told that she would have to wait a few years she informed us that her babysitter, one of the Slonkoskey girls, had a pool in her back yard and already said she would teach her how to swim. Char contacted Slonkoskeys and sure enough, Missie had already talked to the babysitter about it and arrangements were made. By the end of that summer, at the age of three, Missie could swim back and forth four times across the town pool. She became a beautiful swimmer and never made a splash as she swam. She went on to earn her lifesaving certificate at the youngest age permitted at the time.

225. Baton Twirling

When Missie was six she wanted to join Ginny's Ginger Snaps, an area baton twirling group. Everything was fine while she was taking lessons and she was excited to get her costume for the parades. But, once the parades started she was not as interested as she had been. After a particularly long 4th of July parade Missie informed the family that she was no longer going to be in baton. When asked why, she simply stated, "Because I hate to sweat and that is all you do in parades." Missie was told that she would need to finish out the season, which meant two more parades, because she could join or try anything she wanted, but once she joined she was in for that year. Apparently she was very unhappy about those circumstances and the next day packed her little suitcase and sneaked out the back door. Char watched as she was walking down the street and saw her stand at the corner for about ten minutes. Then Missie turned around and came back home. When Char asked what she was doing, Missie said she was running away because she did not want to be in any more parades. Char asked why she came back and Missie said that when she got to the corner she remembered she was not allowed to cross the street by herself so she came home. Two parades later, there was no more baton.

226. Little League Softball

Minster Little League Softball for girls first began when Missie was in grade school and of course she was on one of the first teams. The new program was not the well-oiled machine it is today and many of the girls had no idea how to play ball. Missie had never picked up a bat until her first practice. The attention span of the girls who had never experienced a ballgame before was extremely limited.

In one game, while they were supposed to be playing outfield, Missie and two other girls were sitting down making dandelion chains. That inning they were called in for their turn at bat and given a little pep talk on playing their positions. However, after two more innings of dancing, turning cartwheels and making flower chains while in outfield, the coaches never even bothered to call the girls in for their turn at bat and just allowed them to enjoy their time together. None of the girls realized their team was at bat and had the opposing team's outfielders turning cartwheels with them.

Though sweat was never an issue, there was only one season of softball.

227. Girl Scouts and Dance

Missie thoroughly enjoyed both Girl Scouting and Dance. When she started each of those programs she stayed with them until her early teens. She loved selling cookies and organizing all of the boxes when they came in for delivery. To say that she loved dance would be putting it mildly. Missie somehow managed to dance almost every day of her life in one way or another. As an adult she even tried to talk a local dance instructor into starting adult tap classes.

228. Learning To Be A Saver And Working the Brother's System

Missie dearly loved being a big sister and would never let her baby brothers alone. One time her baby brother Trent was fussing because she would not quit rubbing her hand over his head and down the side of his face. When Char said to stop bothering the baby for a little while, Missie said, "I am not bothering him, I am petting him." She loved being the person in charge.

When Travis and Trent were a few years older Missie would become frustrated when they did not always follow her orders. One day she bribed them with her Halloween candy and from that day forward she saved all the candy from every holiday for bribing purposes. Of course that became a vicious cycle because the boys knew if they did not do what she asked Missie would bribe them. It was apparently a win-win situation for everyone involved.

Besides saving candy, Missie liked saving money. She always wanted to do chores around the house to earn an allowance and she loved to watch the money grow in her bank savings account. Every month she would take her little book to the bank to have them add the few cents interest she had gained. She was all grins and always brought enough suckers home for herself and her three brothers. When we had the tanning studio she would pull the wagon up every day to get the dirty towels and take them back home to wash. She was always looking for a way to add to her savings. As soon as she was old enough to work Missie had a job in New Bremen at Arby's. When she went to college she worked twenty hours a week in Bowling Green's cafeteria and still carried her full course load.

229. Visiting Aunt Anita And Uncle Wally

Missie always had a special connection with her Aunt Anita. Even though Anita literally lived all over the world while Missie was growing up in Minster, somehow they formed a special bond. When Missie was 13-years old she traveled alone, on a direct flight, to visit Aunt Anita and Uncle Wally in Colorado. She was all smiles as she boarded the plane and all smiles when she came home. She had experienced time uninterrupted by parents or brothers and felt as though she had Aunt Anita's undivided attention.

While Missie was in college she and her high school friend, Ellie Bergman, traveled to California to visit Anita and Wally. Apparently Wally and Anita met the girls at the airport and when they arrived home handed them the key to the house, the keys to Aunt Anita's convertible and a map. Once again Aunt Anita had proven she knew just what Missie needed.

230. Missie And Driving

As a young girl, Missie liked to join her dad on Saturday trips to run errands and to the meat market. Missie had only one major deficit in her life. She had absolutely no sense of direction. When first learning to drive she was really okay about finding her way back home as long as she could see the church steeples only half a block from the house. But when she and her girlfriends started to venture outside of Minster it was a different story. This was pre-cell phone days and there were several times that the home phone would ring and it would be Missie calling from some farmer's house along the road asking for directions how to get home or for someone to come and lead her home. When it came to directions and cars, she really was clueless. Missie borrowed her Dad's car one evening. It was a big Lincoln that had side lights. When she and her friends left for a movie it was still daylight. On the way home, in the dark, when using the signal to make a right hand turn, the side lights caused the right ditch to light up. Eventually the girls figured out the light was coming from the turn signal on the side of the car but not before all of them thought they were being followed and someone was shining a flashlight on them.

231. Favorite High School Activities

Missie's favorite activities during high school were the band and school plays. Having danced for several years and being on stage for recitals, she was a natural when it came to appearing before the public. Each year for the band's senior night at the final home game, the seniors chose a younger member of the band to present them with their senior flower at the half-time festivities. Missie would not tell her choice ahead of senior night. While the others received their flowers from buddies and best friends in their section, Missie had chosen to receive her flower from her brother, Travis, a freshman in percussion.

232. Senior Year

As a teenager, Missie was heartbroken when her best friend, Denise, was killed in a car accident just before their senior year. Missie spent hours writing a letter that she wanted to share with Denise forever. While no one knows for sure everything she said, Missie admitted when she had her first daughter and named her Taylor Denise that she was fulfilling a promise she made nine years earlier to her best friend.

After Denise's death Missie began to work with Father Rick Nieberding on programs for young people who had lost loved ones. Father Rick had begun a program a year before called Down On The Farm which invited students from all over Ohio to spend three days on a farm sharing their life experiences with many others like themselves. Missie took great pride in this work and used it throughout her adult life after gaining a degree in psychology and sociology and her Masters in Social Work.

233. Most Clueless

Each year as graduation approaches the senior class votes for students to receive the Senior Superlatives. While others may have been taken back to receive the "Most Clueless" award, Missie relished the recognition. Based on some of the stories shared here, it is easy to understand why she received the superlative. After her daughter was born she even mentioned that perhaps Taylor could someday be a second generation "Most Clueless". Some of Trent's and Ty's favorite Missie stories proves that even as an adult she had some clueless moments.

234. A Ty Memory

This is a typical Missie story from Ty about one day when he was working with her at a day camp.

One summer day we were at Foundations summer day treatment program (the one for the "behaviorally challenged" kids from the surrounding counties). We are all sitting around the room ... myself, a couple other counselors, Mis, and about 18-20 little hellions. We are doing a group exercise. As part of the exercise, each child was asked to think of what plant they would most like to be and to share their choice with the rest of the class, along with an explanation for why they chose the plant they chose. So we start going around the room.

The first little girl says something like, "I want to be a rose, because roses are beautiful!" And Mis, who is leading the exercise, says something like, "Oh how beautiful! A rose! That's great! Alright, how about you Kyle." Kyle says, "I want to be a big tree so that I can see far, far away." And Mis says something like, "Cool! That's great Kyle. Who's next ..."

Then there was a bit of hesitation. Mis did not move too quickly to the next kid, because he was a little different. He was the cream of the crop ... the hellion of the hellions. His name was Shawn, and he was a three-year veteran of the program. Somehow, despite all the chaos he caused each day of each summer he had been there, and despite all the punishment she had to dole out to him, Shawn was one of Mis's favorites. So Shawn was up. Mis said, "Shawn, what would you like to be." Shawn's eyes lit up, he sat up quickly, and immediately replied with an enthusiastic "I a Fungi!" ... pronounced with a long "I" at the end. When Mis heard this she smiled and laughed a bit. She thought he had said "Fun guy," which is the type of thing Shawn would totally say. But that is not what he said or what he meant. He said and he meant "fungi." Meanwhile, I and the other counselors were exchanging smirks, as we knew that Mis is getting the two words confused. Still thinking Shawn had said "Fun Guy," Mis probed further, "Shawn, you are a fun guy! But if you could be any plant, what plant would you be?" And Shawn replied with another enthusiastic long-"I said," "I a Fungi!" Myself and the counselor's smirks immediately turned to bits of subtle laughter. Mis laughed too, this time a little harder and a little shorter and replied again, "Shawn, you are a fun guy!!! You know that!!! But what plant would you like to be?" For the third time, Shawn said enthusiastically--even more enthusiastically than the first two times-- "Fungi!"

Finally, it began to register. Right after he said it you could see the wheels turning in her head. She was putting it together. When it finally dawned on her, she paused for a second, and looked to me and the other counselors for verification. The room was quiet in anticipation. She quickly realized that she was the only one of us who had not caught what Shawn was saying all along. It all came together. And she began laughing. At first it was a normal laugh, but it quickly moved toward harder laughter then elevated to hysterical laughter and then to laughter like I had never heard before! She laughed and laughed! Her laughs were the kind of laughs that you have to laugh at as you watch someone laugh like that. And so the whole room began laughing at her laughs. And then she laughed and laughed some more! We could not tell if she was still laughing about Shawn's response or if now she was laughing because we were laughing! She fell off her chair laughing! We laughed and laughed some more! It was unbelievable! Everyone in the room was laughing, including Mis! For minutes and minutes we laughed and laughed ... the really hard kind of laughing ... the kind that you have to stop for every 10 seconds or so to catch your breath and let your stomach muscles recoup. And we all kept this up ... looking at each other and laughing some more ... until every last drop of laughter we had in us had gotten out. It was spectacular.

235. A Trent Memory

One cold winter day, after Missie and Marc moved to Minster with their two children, she called me and said she had gone home from work sick. She said that as soon as she came from work she went straight back and got in bed. She wanted me to come over because she was still so sick and even colder than when she came home. When I pulled in the driveway I noticed she had left the garage door open. I walked through the garage to her kitchen door and saw that was standing wide open too. She had obviously forgotten to close both doors, it was below zero outside, and it was a straight shot of air to her bedroom at the end of the hall from the kitchen door. When I went back to the bedroom I told her the doors were wide open. Something she said she did not realize.

236. Meeting Her Husband

One weekend Missie and her friends were attending an area festival when one of the girls talked to a few guys standing in a group near them. Missie turned to another friend and asked, "Who is the guy with the dark hair?" Her friend replied, "I think that is Marc Kogge from St. Marys." According to her friends, Missie's response was, "He will be mine. Oh yes, he will be mine!"

And so he was. Missie and Marc were married in April, 1995. They had four children, Wes, Taylor, Andrew and Katie who were the loves of Missie's life. Neighbors have said that every evening after dinner they would hear music turned on and could see Missie in the living room dancing with her young children. Each one of her children was very special to her and she loved being their mother. It was as though she could not hold them or play with them enough.

237. In The End

Missie never wavered too far from the person she was as a little girl. She loved to talk and to be on the go. She loved to be near water. She loved to dance. She loved to organize and be organized. She loved to be in charge. She loved to laugh especially at her own clueless moves. She loved to surprise people with thoughtful cards and gifts. She loved babies and children, especially her own, and she loved family, especially her three brothers. Most importantly, she allowed all those loves in her life to shine through her ever-present smile.

MISSIE

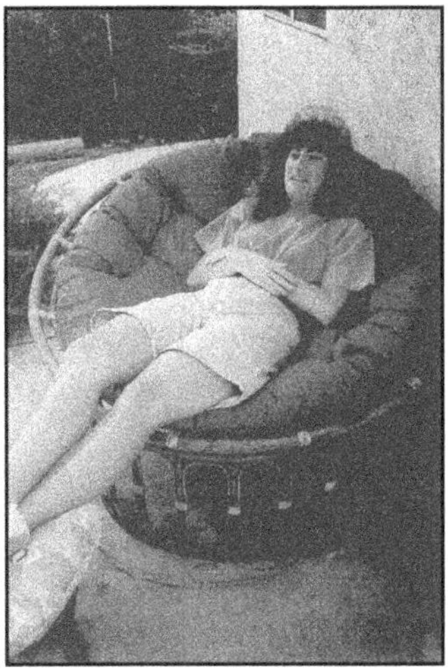

Missie Relaxing On Vacation

Marc And Missie In Their Sunday Best

Missie – Travis – Trent Back Row
Ty – Front Row

Heath – Missie - Lindsay

Trent – Missie – Jerry – Anita

Julie – Missie – Jerry – Trent – Travis

<u>Chapter 9</u>

Final Reflections

238. Reflecting Back

We had summers filled with bike rides, Hula Hoops, baseball, Kool-Aid powder with sugar and large bowls of ice cream at night. On television we watched *Howdy Doody* and the Peanut Gallery, *The Lone Ranger*, *The Shadow*, *The Roy Rogers Show* with – Dale Evens – Nellie Bell – Trigger - Bullet - and Buttermilk. We had Coke-shaped bottles with colored sugar water inside, candy cigarettes, Blackjack – Clove and Teaberry chewing gum, soda pop machines that dispensed real glass bottles. There were newsreels before the movie and PG and R rated movies were not an option. We made decisions by saying 'Eeny-meeny-miney-moe and 'Oly-oly-oxen-free made perfect sense. Mistakes were simply corrected by exclaiming, 'Do it Over.' We would take an entire evening catching lightning bugs. On Saturday morning cartoons we watched real people and we did not have a 30 minute commercial of action figures. Spinning around, getting dizzy, and falling down was the cause for giggles. Baseball cards in the spokes of your bicycle transformed any bike into a motorcycle. Water balloons were the ultimate weapon and our worst embarrassment was being picked last for a team.

During our wonderful childhood days, we had summers filled with bike rides, hay rides or just riding around in our car viewing the local country side. We played baseball in the pasture fields, basketball in the barn and croquet in the yard. We didn't have to be told to get outside and play. This was the natural thing to do. We did not have expensive games to play. We made up games sometimes just to have fun. We would get mad and yell at each other, but we quickly made up because we were taught to love our family. Not going to church every Sunday was not an option and many times Sunday night services were attended. We were taught to tell the truth, be honest, and treat others like we wanted to be treated. Respect for our parents, teachers and grown-ups was expected and practiced.

On television we watched our favorite television programs that were produced with no need to be concerned who the viewer was. We drank Kool-Aid mix with powder and sugar, popped pop corn on the stove and enjoyed large bowls of ice cream at night. Going to a restaurant to eat was a special event. They had tables with table cloths, served plates heaping with food and some even had table side jukeboxes. We drank fresh home pasteurized milk directly from the cow, and home made churned butter on the table. Our bread was delivered directly to our door by the bread man.

We didn't have favorite fast food restaurants. Our food was slow and cooked on the stove at Hathaway Road. When dad got home from work, we sat down together at the kitchen table. If we didn't like what was put on the table we either went away hungry or we had to sit there until we did like it. A prayer from daddy to tell God we were thankful for the food that we were about to eat and the many blessings He had given us that day was a standard at each meal.

The majority of people we knew never set foot on a golf course, traveled out of the country or knew what a credit card was. Pizzas were not delivered to our home, but milk and bread were. There were no movie ratings because all movies were responsibly produced for everyone to enjoy viewing, without profanity or violence or almost anything offensive.

We grew up in the late 50's and the early 60's with practical parents. We had a mother who washed aluminum foil after she cooked in it, then reused it. She was the original recycle queen, before they had a name for it. We had a father who was happier getting old shoes fixed than buying new ones. Their marriage was good, and their dreams were focused. Some of their best friends lived barely a wave away. We can see them now, Dad in trousers, tee shirt and a hat and Mom in a house dress. When it was the time for fixing things around the house, she jumped right in to get the task completed with little help. Things like a curtain rod, a screen door, the oven door, the hem in a dress were not a challenge to our mother. Dad practiced re-fixing, renewing, which was part of his not wanting to be wasteful and throwing things away,

239. The Secrets To The Henkaline Family Success

Our parents taught us to first love God, then love each other and finally love others. They practiced their love to us as a verb and not a noun. You could tell by their actions that their kids were more important than themselves. They somehow knew that teaching us to love each other at a young age would last forever. And it did. They made our family their priority of their lives and gave of themselves to their children with unselfish love and dedication. Our parents taught us to respect them, respect each other and respect others. Their faith encouraged us to trust in God, tell the truth, be honest, be responsible and be faithful in our actions. We were taught to treat others as we wanted to be treated and they guided us by presenting themselves as an extraordinary example of what is right and wrong in God's eyes. We strongly believe that either one of our parents would have given their life to save any one of their children. We also feel any one of the kids would have done the same for Mother and Dad. They made a covenant to be a servant to our needs as long as we lived. Finally they nudged us to have a personal relationship with Jesus Christ, accept his grace and become more like Him.

A Bible passage describing the love our parents showed, what they believed and practiced is found in these passages.

Bible Verses (NKJV) - 1 Corinthians 13: 4 thru 8

Love suffers long and is kind: love does not envy; love does not parade itself, is not puffed up; does not behave rudely, does not seek its own, is not provoked, thinks no evil; does not rejoice in iniquity, but rejoices in the truth; bears all things, believes all things, hopes all things, endures all things. Love never fails.

He loves each of us as if there were only one of us.
St. Augustine

The Henkaline Family In The Early 60's
Jerry – Ken – Jack
Anita – Bill - Olive

William H. and Olive O. Henkaline

WILLIAM H. HENKALINE
August 18, 1906 - August 25, 1983
When I look up into the sky and see the stars so bright...
I'll say a little prayer for you and bid your soul goodnight.

A Tribute To Dad

When I look up into the sky and see the stars so bright. I say a little Prayer for you and I bid your soul goodnight.

A Tribute To Mother

There are many ways to measure Success. The true measurement of person is not what she does on Sunday, but rather who she is on Monday through Saturday.

Chapter 10

Nostalgia

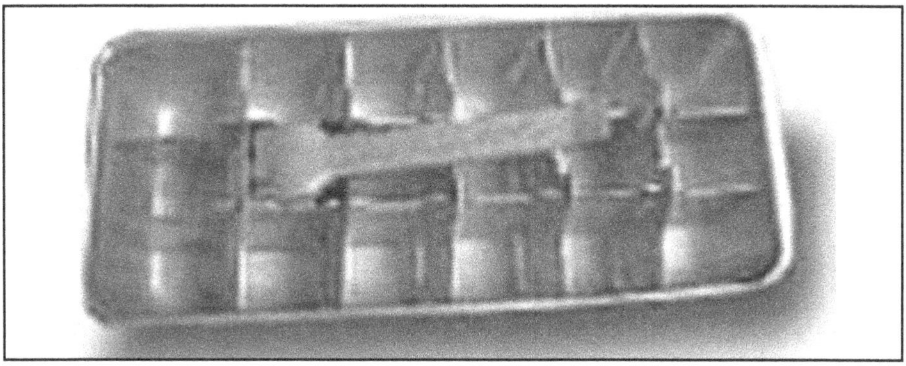

This is a metal ice cube tray we used in our old Refrigerator. There were ice cube compartments with a lever to push for ice cubes removal. To get ice you had to fill the tray, put it into the freezer compartment and wait until it became frozen. Cold water was stored in a glass container on a shelf in the refrigerator. When the water in the container was low you just filled it up again.

This is a roller skate key. The skates were 100% metal including the four wheels. The skates were held on to your shoes by a clamp and the key shown above would be used to tighten the clamp to the shoe. We tried roller skating, in Greenville at our cousin Ann Hittle's house on her sidewalk. We weren't very good at keeping upright.

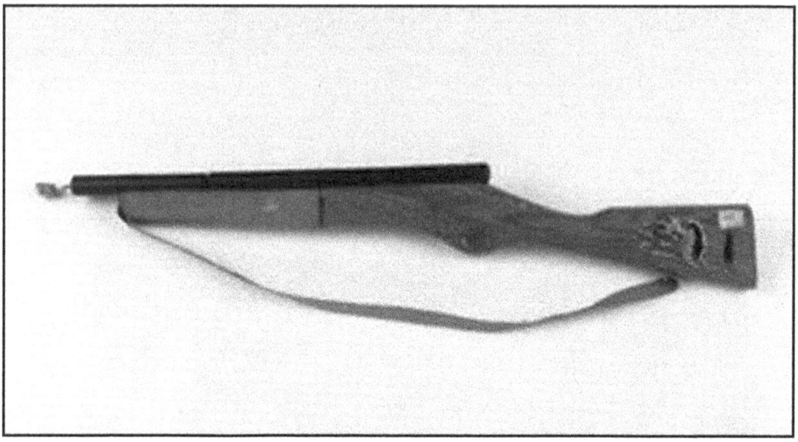

This is a Pop Gun. You pushed the cork into the barrel, pulled the red lever back to get back pressure and pulled the trigger to hear the cork fly out. What fun!

The Greenville, Ohio Drive-In was the outdoor's place to go to see the latest movies. There was an admission per person in the car and usually 2 movies to watch. As teenagers, when we took a car load of boys in with a couple of the boys hiding in the trunk of the car. If you were brave enough to get into the trunk, you would see a free movie. Once in front of the big screen we would pull the car beside a metal post which held a speaker. The speaker was transferred inside your window for listening while you watched the "Big Screen."There was always good food at the concessions stand at intermission.

Greenville A&W root beer stand was a drive up place to get your chilled mug of Root Bear. It was a real treat to get that frosty mug filled with root beer with a Coney dog. Refills were free.

This is a Studebaker car. The bullet front looked like an airplane without the propeller. The model did not catch on very well and the style went back to the traditional look.

We remember this washing machine in the basement of our farm house. The washing machine had a water hose that was hooked up to the hot and cold spickets. There was a drain hose that went to the floor drain and the washing machine was ready to go. Wash day was Monday and Mother would haul the dirty cloths to the washing machine area and separate them into piles. The first pile was put into the tub and the agitator would clean them. Mother would manually stop the wash cycle and run the cloths through the ringer located at the top of the machine. The clothes were then put in a basket and taken to the outside clothes line for drying. Tuesday was ironing day. Mother completed this task for a family of six.

This is a reel tape recorder. We had one and thought it fun to tape conversations. Uncle Francis had a great singing voice and used two recorders like this to put together an all parts production until he compiled a full choir. Back then this was a pretty complex project and his final arrangement sounded pretty good.

This Tinker Toy Erector Set was used to spend many fun hours making sky scrapers, cars, trucks and airplanes using the rods and round spools with holes. Once you built your master piece you just tore it apart and put the parts back into the box.

This Lincoln Log Kit consisted of miniature logs that were notched on the ends to stack and build a play house like the real thing.

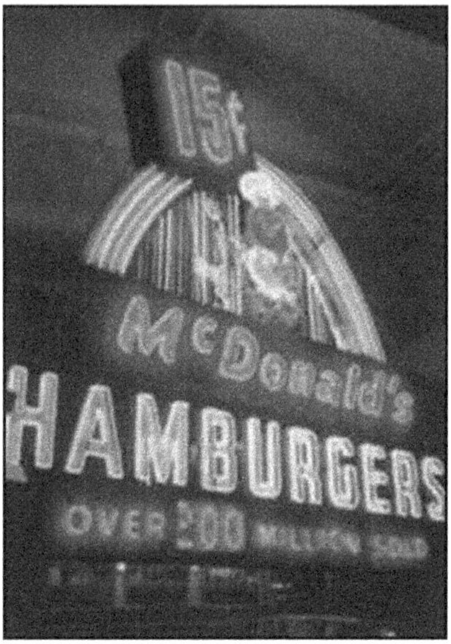

Eating out was a special event. Mc Donald's was the beginning of the fast food chain. A couple of 15 cent hamburgers, fries and a quarter coke would make your meal complete. Ronald Mc Donald came along later in the Mc Donald chain.

Penny candy was a treat that anybody could afford. We received our candy every Friday night when Daddy came home from work. Those were good memories.

Having a baseball card collection was a common thing for a boy in our time. Placing an Earnie Banks or a Mickey Mantle baseball card against your bicycle spokes to make noise as you rode was not unusual. Oh, don't we wish we had those cards today.

Dad worked at a gas station like this in Dayton, Ohio. We can remember gas selling for 25 cents per gallon and the attendant running out as you arrived to fill your tank, wash your windshield and check your oil. Now that was service.

Jiffy Pop was the new generation for making popcorn. You removed the red cover and placed the aluminum container on your stove. As it heated up the aluminum foil would quickly rise and when the corn stopped popping, you removed the aluminum pan from the stove and tore the foil to enjoy a fresh batch of delicious pop corn.

Stamps were only 5 cents when we were growing up.

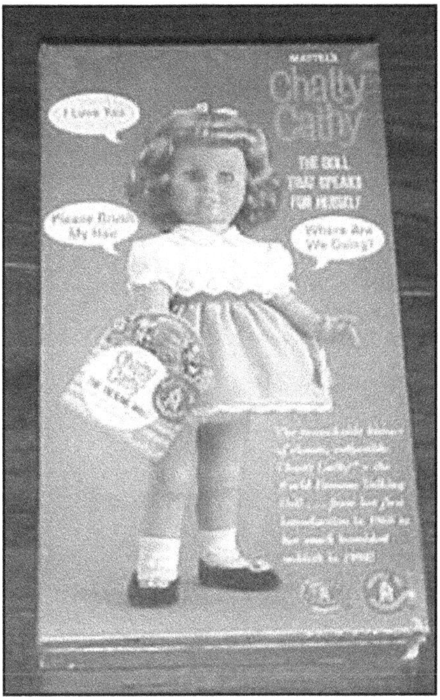

Chatty Cathy was a girl's best friend. She actually talked which delighted her little mother. This doll was the beginning of toy doll innovation.

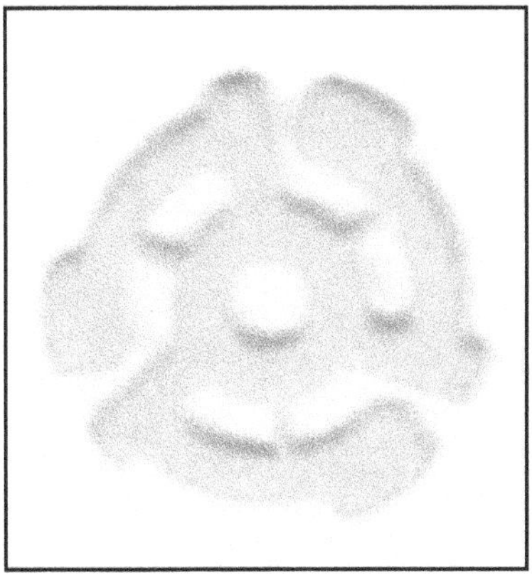

This is a 45 record rpm spindle. It was used to put in the center of your 45 rpm records. The records back then were 33 1/3 and 45 rpm. The record players had a stem in the middle of the rotating plate and 45 rpm records had a big hole. The solution was this little filler.

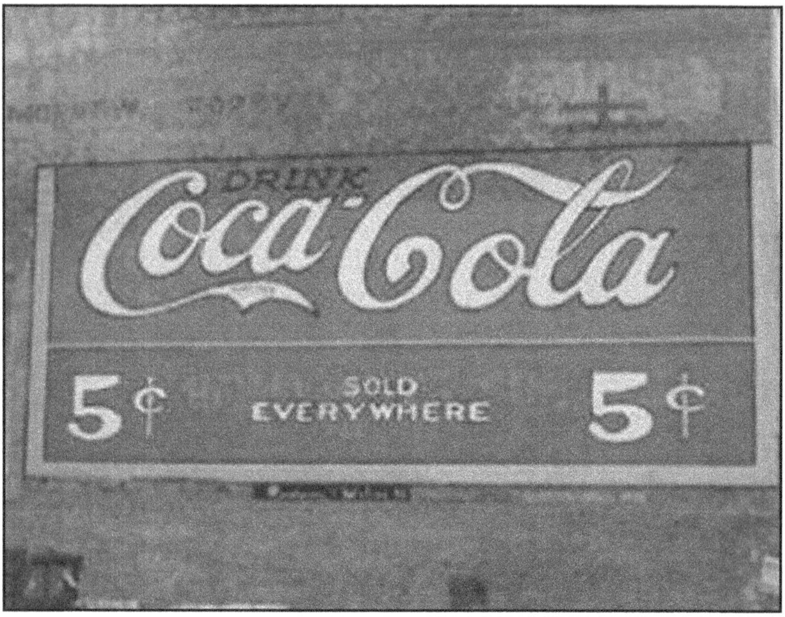

Everybody knows this famous drink. We got our pop for 5 cents for a small 6 ounce bottle and 12 cents for the big 12 ounce bottle.

S&H green stamps were given out at select stores when you made a purchase. You collected the stamps in books and redeemed them for great items like tables, chairs, lamps and other household items.

This little guy was named Speedy Alka-Seltzer. He was your little friend when you had an upset stomach. You just popped two little tablets in a glass of water and Speedy took the pain away.

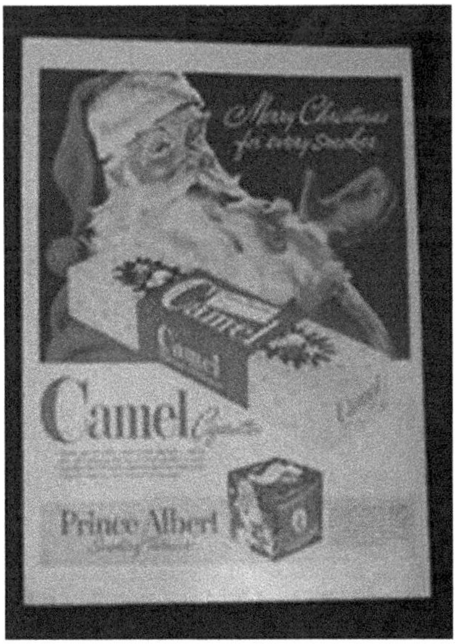

Smoking cigarettes in public places was common to the American people when we grew up. There was never a no-smoking section or restrictions back then. Even on airplanes and confined spaces, people could smoke beside a non smoker and feel comfortable.

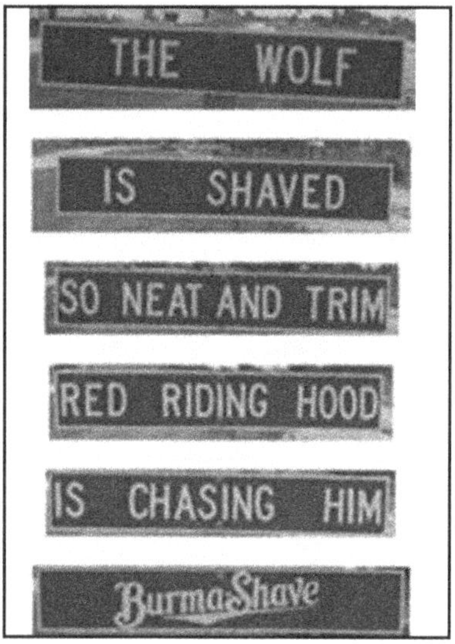

Signs like this could be found all along the highways of rural America. Each sign would be spaced by several hundred feet to attract your attention as you traveled the highway.

The Brownie Camera was the camera we grew up with. It was a box with a lens to view and a lever to push across the top when you felt the time was ready for the picture. No flash bulbs were used with this camera. Putting the roll of film in the camera and taking it out took care to preserve your pictures. You waited a week to see the results after turning the film in to a store.

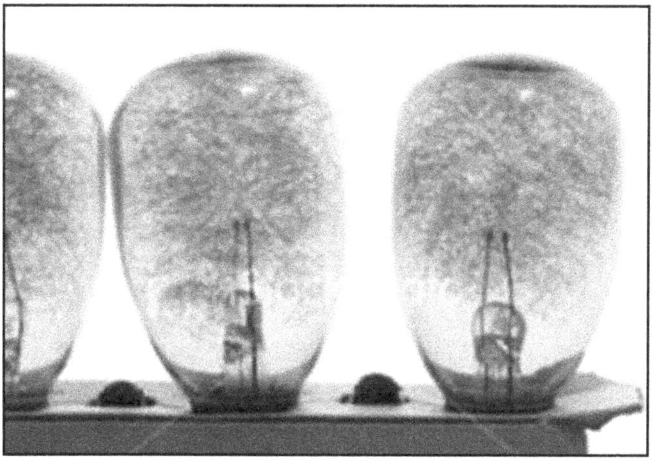

These flash bulbs were the lighting feature for the next generation of cameras.

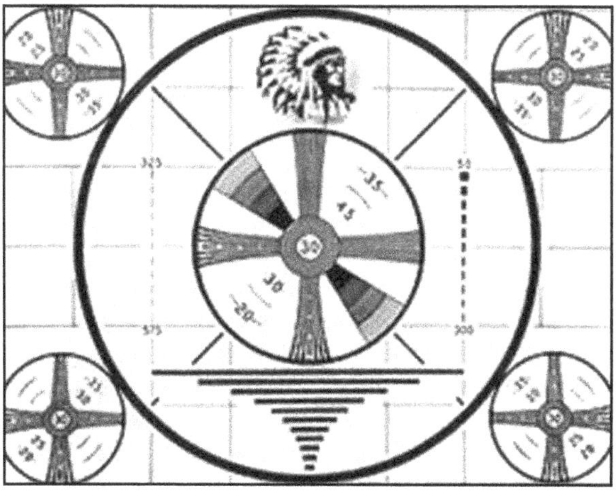

This was common view of your television screen prior to shows being aired, and after the shows went off the air. Television time was restricted to mid morning and continued up to 11:00 pm. There were only 3 networks which were NBC, CBS, and ABC. The television set reception was produced by an external antenna for the rural areas and rabbit ears for large metropolitan areas.

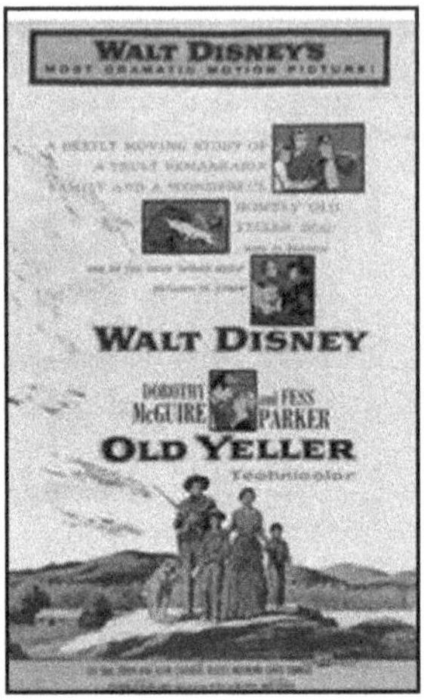

The Walt Disney movie "Old Yeller" was a story about a boy and his dog story. Not many people left the movie house without tears during this powerful adventure. It was a classic that most people in our time saw.

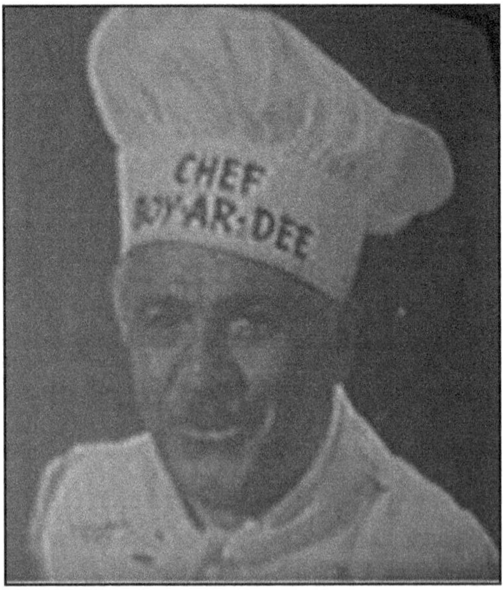

This chef was on the cans of great soups and pastas. He was an icon for great food and his box pizza for home making was an instant hit and he lived in Ohio.

This is an old school house with a Tube Fire Escape. Our Ansonia school house had exterior steel platforms and steps to escape. Thankfully we only had to use them during fire drills.

Timmy and Lassie were among the best of the television series. The show played every Sunday night. We missed some shows because we were forced to go to the Sunday night church service. Lassie was our K-9 hero.

Ding-Dong....Avon Calling was a new career adventure for the woman of our time. A lady could use this part time sales position to help meet the family budget. It was a well respected sales position.

Brylcreem...A little dab will do ya. That was the theme of this hair cream for men. After applying, your hair would get the wet look that all men were looking for.

All girls in gym had ugly uniforms

It took three minutes for the television to warm up so we could see a picture. The inside was full of large and small tubes.

Nobody in our neighborhood owned a purebred dog

A Quarter was a decent weekly allowance.

We would reach in a muddy gutter for a penny.

You got your windshield cleaned, your oil checked and gas pumped without asking. This service was all for free, every time and you never had to pay for air to put in your tires. Trading stamps were also given as a bonus.

Laundry detergent had free glasses, dishes or towels hidden in the box.

The Aluminum Christmas Tree. This sporty tree was easy to put up and take down. You could use it year after year and the colored disk wheel transformed the aluminum branches to vibrant color in repeated series. The Henkaline family fell for this sales pitch and had a tree like this one for several years. The artificial Christmas green tree finally took its place after a few years.

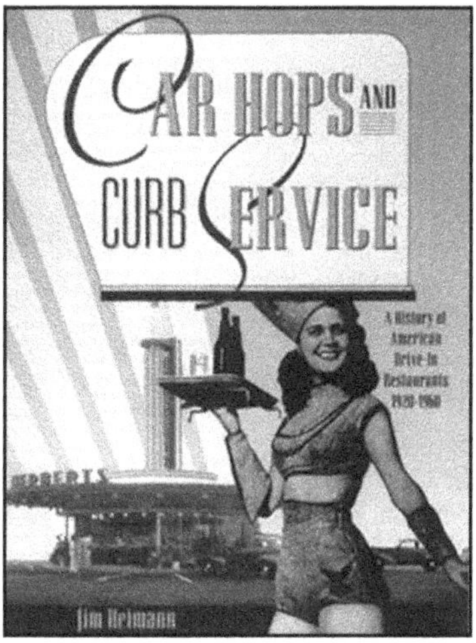

It was a REAL TREAT to be taken to a drive-in diner or a real restaurant with your parents

The teacher threatened to keep kids back a grade if we didn't pass the test. And they did it!

A 1957 Chevy was everyone's dream car…to cruise, peel out, and lay rubber.

No one ever asked where the car keys were because they were always in the car and in the ignition. The doors were never locked.

Lying on your back in the grass and looking at the clouds was a common pastime. When you had friends with you…you would say things like, "That cloud looks like a . . .

Playing baseball with your friends in the backyard or field was great fun.

Stuff from the store came without safety caps and hermetic seals because no one tried to poison a perfect stranger.

Sitting on the swing on a hot day with your family was a fun thing to do. Family members could just sit back, and savor the slow pace and share good times.

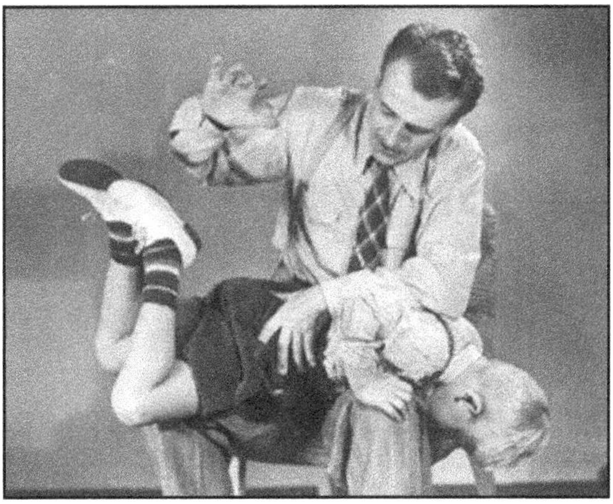

Being sent to the principal's office was nothing compared to the fate that awaited you when you got home. The spanking was done in love for respect and behavior and we knew this.

Sometimes we were in fear for our lives, but it wasn't because of drive-by shootings, drugs or gangs. Our parents were a much bigger threat! But we survived because their love was greater than the threat.

Chapter 11

In Closing

All the stories told are the Henkaline Kids' memories of our childhood. They began with a family full of love that began in a House that turned into a Home on Hathaway Road near Woodington, Ohio. Our memories will never go away. It's been fun telling and explaining our time and experiences growing up in a beautiful home provided by our wonderful and loving parents. We hope this book inspires you to take the time to write your own book of your family and experiences growing up. God Bless You and Your Family.

Anita *Jerry* *Jack* *Ken*

CHAPTER 12

The Henkaline Family Tree

FAMILY GROUP NUMBER	HUSBAND's FULL NAME: William Henry Henkaline		
This Information Obtained From:	Husband's Date	Day Month Year	City, Town, Place County or Province State or Country
	Birth	18 Aug. 1906	
Family Information	Married	29 Nov. 1935	Portland, Indiana
Family Tree Documents - Marion Craig	Death	25 Aug. 1983	Greenville, Ohio - Darke County
	Burial		Ansonia Cemetery, Ansonia, Ohio - Darke County
	Place of Residence		RR#1 Hathaway Road, Ansonia, Ohio - Darke County
	Occupation		Factory Worker and Farmer Church Affiliation: Protestant - Military Record: None
	His Father	John Henry	Mother's Maiden Name: Pearl May Foreman
	Wife's FULL NAME: Olive Opal Henkaline (Hittle)		
Compiler: Jack B. Henkaline	Wife's Date	Day Month Year	City, Town, Place County or Province State or Country
1081 Chippewa Drive	Birth	14-Dec-09	
Van Wert, Ohio - Van Wert County	Married	29 Nov. 1935	Portland, Indiana
Date: 15-Jul-2011	Death	18-Apr-84	Greenville, Ohio - Darke County
	Burial		Ansonia Cemetery, Ansonia, Ohio - Darke County
	Place of Residence		RR#1 Hathaway Road, Ansonia, Ohio
	Occupation		Housewife - Church Affiliation: Protestant
This Information Obtained From:	Her Father	Henry Hittle	Mother's Maiden Name: Sarah (Sadie) Hittle
Children's Names in Fill (Arrange in order of Birth)	Children's Date	Day Month Year	City, Town, Place County or Province State or Country
1	Birth	14-Jan-1938	**Children**
Anita Louise			580 Juniper Street
	Married	25-Oct-1968	Chula Vista - California - 91911
Name	Death		**Beverly**
	Burial		**Keith**
Wallace K. Pearson	Birth	14-May-1932	**Kenneth**
Name Of Spouse	Married	25-Oct-1968	Calvary Temple - Denver, Colorado
	Death		
	Burial		
2			
Joyce Ann	Birth	23-Sep-1943	Ansonia, Ohio - Darke County
Name	Married		
	Death	24-Oct-1943	
	Burial		Ansonia Ohio Cemetery - Darke County
Name Of Spouse			
3			
Jerry Wayne	Birth	15-Aug-1945	17B Eagle Drive - Minster, Ohio 45865
Name	Married	30-Aug-1969	**Missie**
	Death		**Travis**
	Burial		**Trent**
Charlene Henkaline (Fullenkamp)	Birth	11-Sep-1948	**Ty**
Name Of Spouse	Married	30-Aug-1969	
	Death		
	Burial		
4			
Jack Blaine	Birth	18-Aug-1947	1081 Chippewa Drive, Van Wert, Ohio - Van Wert County
Name	Married	12-Aug-1966	**Christopher**
	Death		
	Burial		
Sharon Terue Henkaline (Brown)	Birth	5-Dec-1946	
Name Of Spouse	Married	12-Aug-1966	
	Death		
	Burial		
5			
Kenneth Gene	Birth	12-Jan-1949	1206 Maplewood Drive - Piqua, Ohio 45356
Name	Married	28-Mar-1981	**Heather**
	Death		**Heath**
	Burial		**Lindsay**
Julia Lee Henkaline (Fess)	Birth	30-Jul-1957	**Mark**
Name Of Spouse	Married	28-Mar-1981	
	Death		
	Burial		

FAMILY GROUP NUMBER	HUSBAND's FULL NAME: **Henry Henkaline**		
This Information Obtained From:	Husband's Date	Day Month Year	City, Town, Place County or Province State or Country
	Birth	20 Dec. 1849	Miamisburg, Ohio - Montgomery County
St. Jacob's	Married	23 Dec. 1875	Miamisburg, Ohio
Evangelical Lutheran Church	Death	10 Oct. 1919	Greenville, Ohio - Darke County
Miamisburg, Ohio	Burial		Greenville Cemetery
Old Church Records	Place of Residence		Miamisburg and Greenville
	Occupation		Farmer - Church Affiliation: Lutheran - Military Record: None
Mathias and Agatha Stocker	Other wives, if any		
were born in Watenburg, Germany	His Father	Leonard Henkaline	Mother's Maiden Name | Cristina
He was a Blacksmith in 1870			
Census Record	**Wife's FULL NAME: Anna Stocker**		
Compiler: Marion Craig	Wife's Date	Day Month Year	City, Town, Place County or Province State or Country
11831 Pearl Road	Birth	12 Jan. 1853	Lancaster County - Pennsylvania
Strongsville, Ohio	Married		Greenville, Ohio - Darke County
Date: February 28, 1986	Death	06 May. 1923	
	Burial		Greenville Cemetery
	Place of Residence		Pennsylvania, Miamisburg, Greenville
	Occupation		Housewife - Church Affiliation: Lutheran
	Other husbands, if any		
This Information Obtained From:	Her Father	Mathias Stocker	Mother's Maiden Name: Agatha Stocker
Children's Names in Fill (Arrange in order of Birth)	Children's Date	Day Month Year	City, Town, Place County or Province State or Country
1	Birth	07 Apr. 1876	Miamisburg, Ohio - Montgomery County
John Henry	Married		
Name	Death	15 Aug. 1943	Dayton, Ohio
	Burial		Greenville, Ohio - Darke County
Pearl Foreman	Birth		
Name Of Spouse	Married		
	Death		
2	Burial		
Clarence Edward	Baptized	May. 1877	Miamisburg Lutheran Church
Name	Married		
	Death		
Unknown	Burial		
Name Of Spouse			
3			
George Matheus	Baptized	1881	
Name	Married	04 Jan. 1912	
	Death		
Elizabeth Rehmert	Burial		
Name Of Spouse			
Dora (Cora) Angnes	Baptized	26 May 1881	Miamisburg, Ohio Lutheran Church
Name Of Spouse	Married		
4			
Andrew	Birth		
Name	Married		Greenville, Ohio
	Death		Greenville, Ohio
Anna	Burial		
Name Of Spouse	Birth		
	Married		
	Death		
5	Burial		
William	Birth		
Name	Married		
	Death		
	Burial		
Name Of Spouse	Birth		
	Married		
	Death		
	Burial		
6			
Charlie	Birth		Greenville, Ohio
Name	Married		
	Death		
	Burial		
Bessie	Birth	28 Oct. 1892	Greenville, Lutheran Church
Name Of Spouse	Married		
	Death	1978	Dayton, Ohio
	Burial		

FAMILY GROUP NUMBER	HUSBAND's FULL NAME: John Henry Henkaline		
This Information Obtained From:	Husband's Date	Day Month Year	City, Town, Place County or Province State or Country
	Birth	07 Apr. 1876	Miamisburg, Ohio - Montgomery County
St. Jacob's	Chr'nd		St. Jacobs Ev Lutheran Church
Evangelical Lutheran Church	Married		
Miamisburg, Ohio	Death	15 Aug. 1943	Dayton, Ohio
	Burial		Greenville, Ohio - Darke County
Old Church Records	Place of Residence		Darke County, Ansonia, Ohio and Dayton Ohio
	Occupation		Farmer - Church Affiliation Christian - Military Record None
Henry Foreman was a relative who	Other wives, if any		
was part Indian.	His Father		Henry Henkaline - Mothers Maiden Name: Anna Stocker
He was adopted by a white family			
	Wife's FULL NAME: Pearl May Foreman		
Compiler: Marion Craig	Wife's Date	Day Month Year	City, Town, Place County or Province State or Country
11831 Pearl Road	Birth	01 Jul. 1885	
Strongsville, Ohio	Chr'nd		
Date: April 24, 1981	Married	04 Aug. 1957	Greenville, Ohio - Darke County
	Death		Ansonia Cemetery
	Burial		Darke County, Ansonia, Ohio and Dayton Ohio
	Occupation		Housewife Church Affiliation: Christian
	Other husbands, if any		Otto Summers
	Her Father	Henry Foreman	Mother's Maiden Name: Margaret Lephart

	Children's Date	Day Month Year	City, Town, Place County or Province State or Country	Children
1				
Nellie	Birth	18 Feb. 1902	Greenville, Ohio - Darke County	
Name	Married			
	Death	14 Aug. 1970	Woodington, Ohio, Darke County	**Thurman**
Charlie Shivedecker	Burial		Beamsville Cemetery, Darke County	**James**
Name Of Spouse				
2				
Stanley Anderson	Birth	29 Jan. 1904		**Don**
Name	Married	03 Apr. 1926		**Robert**
	Death			**Janet**
	Burial			**Barbara**
Fern Beatrice Hittle			Fathers Name: Albert Hittle - Children: Alfred - 1906; Fern: 1907; - Russel - 1908; LaVina - 1912; Pauline - 1914; Leona - 1922	
Name Of Spouse			Mothers Maiden Name: Fanny Derr	
3				
William Henry	Birth	18 Aug. 1906		**Anita**
Name	Married	29 Nov. 1935		**Joyce**
	Death	25 Aug. 1983		**Jerry**
	Burial		Ansonia Cemetery, Darke County, Ohio	**Jack**
Olive Opal Hittle				**Kenneth**
Name Of Spouse				
4				
John Milton	Birth	27 Feb. 1911		**Kevin**
Name	Married	26 Jul. 1930		**Carole**
	Death	01 Mar. 1973		**Michael**
	Burial		Strongsville, Ohio, Cuyahoga., County	**Thomas**
Marian Mc Kay				
Name Of Spouse				
5				
Harriet Pearl	Birth	27 Aug. 1908	Greenville, Ohio	
Name	Death	10 Aug. 1909		
	Burial		Greenville, Ohio Cemetery, Darke County	
6				
Mary Magdalene	Birth	07 Feb. 1918	Greenville, Ohio	
Name	Death	07 Feb. 1918	Greenville, Ohio Cemetery, Darke County	
	Burial			
7				
Roger Wayne	Birth	22 Feb. 1923	Ansonia, Ohio, Darke County	**Susan**
Name	Married		California	**Sandra**
	Death			**Steven**
	Burial			
Gertrude Ann Coats				
Name Of Spouse				

FAMILY GROUP NUMBER	**HUSBAND's FULL NAME: Leonard Henkaline**		
This Information Obtained From:	Husband's Date	Day Month Year	
	Birth	Ca 1818	Wertenburg. Germany
Found deed to property. It was at the	Chr'nd		
south east corner of the mound in	Married		
Miamisburg, Ohio.	Death	Ca 1863 to 6	
Account needed of a legal audit	Burial		
	Place of Residence		Miamisburg, Ohio - Montgomery County, Miami
Census 1850	Occupation		
1870	Other wives, if any		
In Fort Wayne, Indiana	His Father		
	Wife's FULL NAME: Cristina		
Compiler: Marion Craig	Wife's Date	Day Month Year	
11831 Pearl Road	Birth		Germany
Strongsville, Ohio	Chr'nd		
Date: March 5, 1986	Married		
	Death		
	Burial		Germany, Miamisburg, Ohio
	Occupation		
	Other husbands, if any		
	Her Father		
	Children's Date	Day Month Year	City, Town, Place County or Province State or Country Children
1	Birth	20 Dec. 1849	Miamisburg, Ohio - Montgomery County
Henry Henkaline Name	Married	23 Dec. 1875	Miamisburg, Ohio - Montgomery County
	Death	10 Oct. 1919	Greenville, Ohio - Darke County
	Burial		
Anna Stocker			
Name Of Spouse			

Ancestor Chart

Name of Compiler
Marian Craig
11831 Pearl Road #611
Strongsville, Ohio
2/26/11

b	b. Date of Birth
p.d.	p.b. Place of Birth
m.	m. Date of Marriage
p.m.	p.m. Place of Marriage
d	d. Date of Death
p.d.	p.d. Place of Death

4	**Henry Henkaline**
b.	20 -Dec-1849
p.b.	Miamisburg, Ohio
m.	23-Dec-1875
p.m.	Miamisburg, Ohio
d.	10 Oct. 1919
p.d.	Greenville, Ohio - Darke County

8	**Leonart Henkaline**
b.	1818
p.b.	
m.	
p.m.	
d.	ca 1863 - 6
p.d.	

16	
b.	
m.	
d.	

17	
b	
d	

2	**John Henry Henkaline**
b.	7-Apr-1876
p.b.	Miamisburg, Ohio
m.	
p.m.	
d.	15-Aug-1943
p.d.	Dayton, Ohio - Montgomery County

9	**Cristina**
b.	1815
p.b.	
m.	
p.m.	
d.	
p.d.	

18	
b.	
m.	
d.	

19	
b	
d	

5	**Anna Stocker**
b.	12-Jan-1853
p.b.	Lancaster County, Penn.
m.	
p.m.	
d.	6-May-1927
p.d.	Greenville, Ohio

10	**Mathias Stocker**
b.	1824
p.b.	Wertenberg, Germany
m.	
p.m.	
d.	1904 Miamisburg, Ohio
p.d.	Miamisburg Cemetery

20	
b.	
m.	
d.	

21	
b	
d	

	William Henry Henkaline
b.	18-Aug-06
p.b.	Greenville, Ohio - Darke County
m.	29-Nov-35
p.m.	
d.	25-Aug-1983
p.d.	Ansonia, Ohio - Darke County

11	**Agatha**
b.	1829
p.b.	Wertenberg, Germany
m.	
p.m.	
d.	1904
p.d.	Miamisburg, Ohio

22	
b.	
m.	
d.	

23	
b	
d	

6	**Henry Foreman**
b.	18-Aug-1858
p.b.	
m.	
p.m.	
d.	1-Jan-1935
p.d.	

12	
b.	
p.b.	
d.	
p.d.	

24 - 25	
b.	
m.	
d.	

13	
b.	
p.b.	
d.	
p.d.	

26 - 27	
b	
d	

3	**Pearl Mae Foreman**
b.	1-Jul-1884
p.b.	
m.	
p.m.	
d.	4-Aug-1959
p.d.	Greenville, Ohio - Darke County

14	**Henry Lephart**
b.	15-Jul-1843
p.b.	Somerset County, Penn
m.	19-Nov- 1863
p.m.	Darke County, Ohio
d.	17-Aug-16
p.d.	Ansonia Cemetery

28	**Augustus Lephart**
b.	27-Dec-1818
p.b.	Near Wald Kappole, Germany
m.	12-Sept-1840
d.	14-Nov-09
p.d.	Greenville, Ohio - Barie Hill

3	**Margaret Adeline Lephart**
b.	2-Jun-1864
p.b.	Ansonia, Ohio - Darke County
m.	
p.m.	
d.	
p.d.	

29	**Katherine E. St Staukoff**
b.	1-Feb-1814
p.b.	Near Wald Kappole, Germany
d.	1 Jan-1816
p.d.	Greenville, Ohio - Barie Hill

30	**Michael Moyer**
b.	
p.b.	
m.	
p.m.	
d.	
p.d.	

Pearl Foreman's Sisters and Brothers

* Emma Schafer	Effie Knee
Sara Jones	James - M. Iva
Dorothy Shafer	Irene
Margaret Jones	Nettie Miller
William	Mena Bliss (Earl's Wife)
Earl	Thomas
	Glenn
* Daughter of Emma	Kate

Nora Garrison - Oxford, Ohio

Henry Henkaline's Sisters and Brothers

George	William
Charley	Cora (Baptized May 23, 1881)
Andrew	Bessie
Edward (Baptized May 26, 1876)	

George and Elizabeth Henkaline

Married 1 January 1912 at the Lutheran Church in Greenville, Ohio - Darke County

Their Children

Anna Noreen	Married - Caupp - Moved To Dayton, Ohio
Birth: 20-Mar 1913	
Baptized: 1-Jun-1913	
Confirmed: 23-Aug-1925	

Dortha Lea
Birth: 10-Oct-1918
Baptized: 19-Jan-1919
Conformed:9-Apr-1933

Paul Eugene
Birth: 5 Dec-1921
Baptized: 18-Jun-1922
Conformed:

George Rieter
Birth: 9 Feb-1930
Baptized: 20-July-1930
Conformed:

Mary Louise
Birth:
Married Steinhiler - 4-Mar-1939 at Church)
Conformed: 31-Mar-1929

AUGUST Lephart

Second Wife - Married: 3-May-1887

Margaret Barbara Serentz	
Birth: 25-Apr. 1825	Justis Lephart Father
Death: 23-Jun. 1899	
Burried: Greenville, Cemetery	Elizabeth A Kraus Mother

www.ingramcontent.com/pod-product-compliance
Lightning Source LLC
Chambersburg PA
CBHW020511100426
42813CB00030B/3199/J
* 9 7 8 1 5 9 3 3 0 8 1 2 4 *